MEMOIk

CONCERNING THE

FRENCH SETTLEMENTS

AND

FRENCH SETTLERS

IN THE COLONY OF

RHODE ISLAND

By
ELISHA R. POTTER

CLEARFIELD

Originally published as
Rhode Island Historical Tracts, No. 5
Providence, Rhode Island, 1879

Reprinted by
Genealogical Publishing Company
Baltimore, Maryland, 1968

Library of Congress Catalog Card Number 68-27007

Reprinted for
Clearfield Company by
Genealogical Publishing Company,
Baltimore, Maryland, 1996, 2012

ISBN 978-0-8063-02805

Made in the United States of America

Sam.l Bennet

John Aylesworth

W.m Weaver

Thos Fry

Joseph Cory

P. Tillinghast.

JOHNSON CORNERS

Elisha Johnson 21 a.

Samuel Bennet.

Matteson. 23¾ a

D.r Briggs. 100 ½ a.

Pardon Tillinghast's Farm.

108 ¾ a

Site of P. Tillinghast's House 102 a.

Joshua Davis 103 a.

William Wanton.

N

251 a.

Col. Peter Money

Line between Kingstown and East Greenwich

FRENCH ORCHARD.

Spring

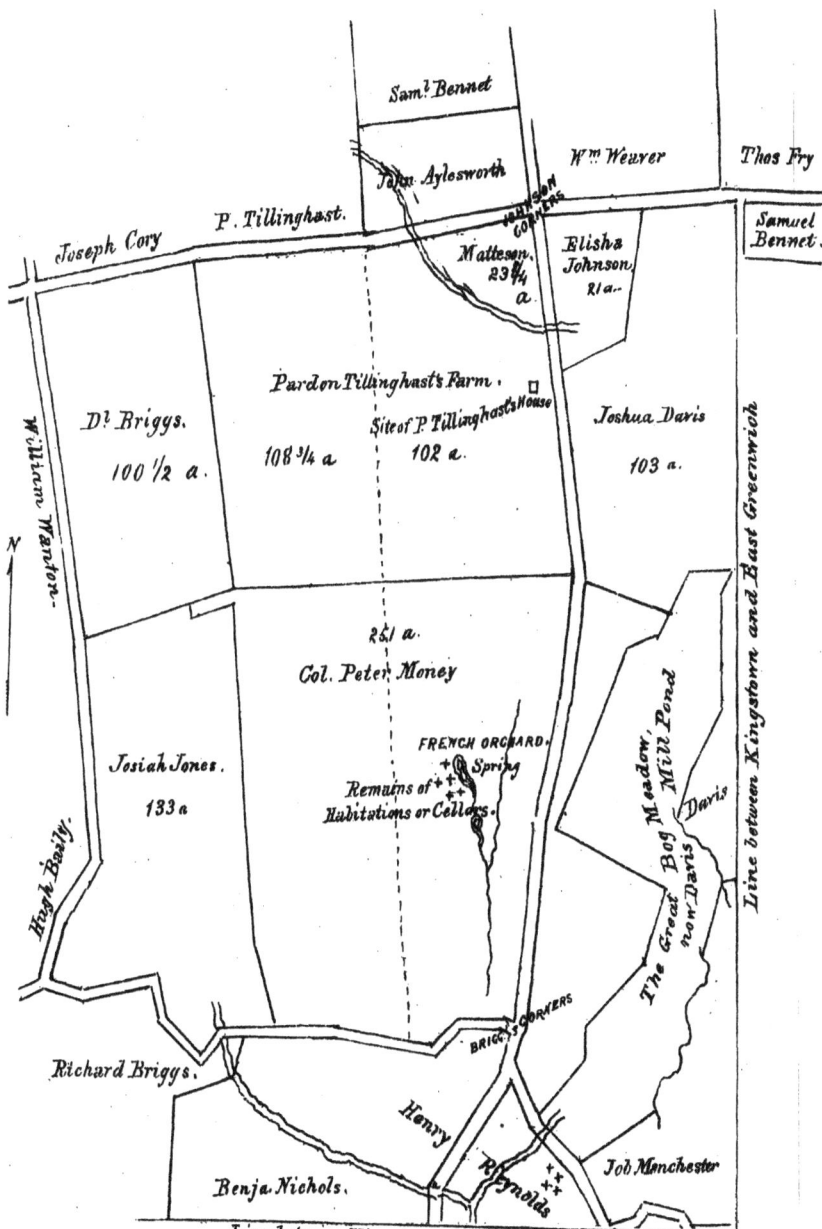

Remains of Habitations or Cellars.

Josiah Jones. 133 a

High Banly.

The Great Bog Meadow. Mill Pond

Davis

now Davis

BRIGGS CORNERS

Richard Briggs.

Henry Reynolds

Job Manchester

Benja. Nichols.

Line between Kingstown and East Greenwich

Remains of Habitations +++

PRELIMINARY MEMOIR.

OF the numerous French settlements in America,
those in Canada, Maine, and some others, probably
had their origin in the love of enterprise and adven-
ture. But the motives which produced the settlements in Rhode Island, Massachusetts, and the south-
eastern States, were, in a great measure, religious.
The reformation which took place in the sixteenth
century was attended with almost unceasing wars
and civil convulsions. The principle of tolerating
all religious opinions to the utmost limit consistent
with the preservation of public morality and order,
was then almost unknown. Religion was regarded
by all governments as a part of the machinery of
state, and to attack the established church was of
course rebellion against the powers that were.

The Lutheran reformation soon spread over

Europe. In France the protestants were generally known by the name of Huguenots. The origin of this name is not certainly known.

In 1562 the dissensions between the two religious parties in France had arisen to such a height that an open war broke out between them. The Catholic party for the greater part of the time from the beginning of the troubles until the repeal of the Edict of Nantes and the expulsion of the protestants from France, had the advantage of having all the power of the civil government exerted in their favor. The war continued with more or less violence until 1572 when the leaders of the protestant party having been invited to Paris on pretence of bringing about a general reconciliation, the ever memorable massacre of St. Bartholomew took place. In this massacre seventy thousand protestants, including almost all the leaders of the party, fell victims to the bloody spirit of religious persecution.

The Catholics in France and at Rome celebrated this event with thanksgivings and jubilees, and medals were struck to commemorate their victory.

This massacre took place in the reign of Charles

the Ninth, and during the remainder of his reign the conscientious protestants enjoyed no rest. Henry the Third, who was supposed to favor protestantism, was assassinated in 1589. Henry the Fourth succeeded, and quiet was restored to the nation for a time.

Henry the Fourth, who before his coming to the throne of France had been King of Navarre, had been educated a protestant, and was naturally inclined to favor their cause. On his accession, from motives of policy, the greater part of his subjects being attached to the Church of Rome, he made a public profession of the Catholic religion, but he was of too enlarged a mind to lend himself to be the instrument of oppression to any party and to endanger the peace of France and the stability of the government, by a vain endeavor to produce a uniformity of religious opinion.

In the year 1598 he published the celebrated Edict of Nantes, so called from the city of Nantes where it was signed. By this a free toleration was granted to the protestants in matters of religious opinion; the offices of the state were made accessible to them;

funds were allowed them for the maintenance of their worship; and for a further security to them against the malice of their persecuting foes and against any sudden change of policy in the government, certain cities were assigned to them as places of refuge and defence.

The giving to the protestants the control of certain portions of the kingdom seems inconsistent with all modern notions of religious freedom. It may have been justified by the turbulent state of the times. But it laid the foundation of much of the subsequent troubles.

During the whole of this prince's reign the terms of the Edict were faithfully adhered to. He perished by assassination in 1610, and with him the hopes of the protestants for security in time to come.

During the succeeding reign of Louis the Thirteenth, the Edict of Nantes was several times solemnly reaffirmed, and the confirmation by Louis the Thirteenth, dated March 12, 1615, is especially remarkable for its expressions of liberality and toleration of religious differences.

Had the protestants been governed by wise and

moderate counsels, their fate might have been different. But they bitterly assailed Henry the Fourth, for his change of religion, and they suffered themselves to become the victims and tools of ambitious nobles whose only motive was to obtain power in the state for themselves. The ambition of the nobles to control the government was, for several generations, the source of almost constant civil war, and although religion was generally the pretext, yet it was sometimes merely a pretence, and frequently not unmixed with political motives. Louis the Thirteenth laid siege to Rochelle, which had become practically almost independent,* and it was compelled to surrender in 1629. But even then the free exercise of their religion was guaranteed to them by the Edict of Grace, signed by Cardinal Richelieu.†

But the strength of the Huguenots as a party was now broken, and in 1685 Louis the Fourteenth, under the influence of the clergy, repealed the Edict of Nantes. The open profession of the reformed religion was prohibited, the ministers of the reformed

---

* Weiss's History of the French Protestant Refugees, i., 48.

† Weiss's 　 " 　 " 　 " 　 " 　 " 　 i., 48, 50.

faith compelled to leave the kingdom, and a series of persecutions commenced which drove away from their country a large proportion of the reformed; in effect, all those who preferred the enjoyment of their own religious opinions to compliance with the religion of the state. This was a blow to the prosperity of France from which it was long in recovering. The persecuted fled to England, Holland, Geneva, Brandenburgh and America. The number has been variously estimated; sometimes as high as a million. They were not of the poorer or more ignorant classes of society. They comprised within their ranks a large portion of the wealth, intelligence, and enterprise of the country, and were gladly welcomed by the nations to which they fled, as a valuable acquisition not only to their numbers, but to their intellectual resources and manufacturing industry.

Those who settled at New Rochelle in the State of New York, in New York city, on the James River in Virginia, on the Santee River and in Charleston, South Carolina, came over during the troubles which preceded and followed the revocation of the Edict of

Nantes, and from the same motives which prompted
the settlements made in Massachusetts and Rhode
Island. Among their descendants were many who
took an active part in our American Revolution, and
who were otherwise distinguished as statesmen or
public benefactors. It will suffice to mention the
names of Jay, Laurens, Manigault, Marion, and
Boudinot.

Within a few years after the repeal of the Edict,
the settlement in Massachusetts was made by about
thirty French families. They received a grant of ten
or twelve thousand acres of land in the township of
Oxford, from the proprietors of the township, and
there they continued to live and the settlement flour-
ished until about 1696, when, harassed by attacks
from the Indians and the settlers, they were scattered over the country. Most of them went to Boston. As they had fled to this country for the sake
of religious opinion, it may naturally be supposed
that after their arrival here, they would maintain and
respect the ordinances of religion. While at Oxford
they maintained a minister of their own sect, and
when they had removed to Boston they built and for

a long time supported a church in which services were performed in their vernacular tongue. Here, as elsewhere, they and their descendants were of respectable condition in society, and some have left behind them good and great names which will long be remembered. For a more particular account of this settlement reference may be made to a very able and learned Essay on the History of the French Protestants, by Rev. Abiel Holmes of Cambridge.*

* Massachusetts Historical Collections, volume xxii.

Wm Barbut	Est	
Paul Collin	Bertin dit Laronde	
Jean Germon	Menardeau	
Dechamps	Galay	MEADOW
fougere	Ratier	GROUND
Grignon	Dauid	
Legaré	Beauchamps	
Robineau	Moize le Brun	

The great Road that leads between the Home lots that leads to the great plaines & to the way to Boston

Petter Aynault	La terre pour l'Eglise	
Magni Junior	La terre pour L'ecolle	
Magni Senior	Le Broton	
Dauid Junior	Le Vigne	
Dauid Senior	Tauerrier	
Chadene	Bouniot	
foretier	Lemoine	
Ezechiel Carré Ministre	Abraum tourtellot	
Louis Alaire	La Veue Colay	
Jamain	Targé Junior	
Russereau	Targé Senior	
Grasilier	Arnaud	
Amian	Lambert	
Lafon	Rambert	
Belhair	Coudret	
Milard		
Jouet	Jean Jullien	
Renaud		
Le vendre	Ouest	

THE GREAT RIVER RUNNING TO THE EST

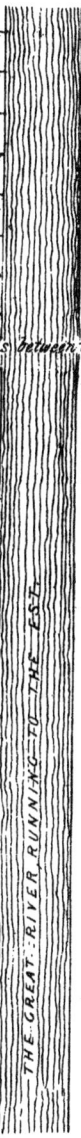

The great Road running by the river into the woods

The great Lots belonging to the Home lots

Sud.

THE FRENCHTOWN SETTLEMENT.

OCTOBER 12, 1686, Richard Wharton, Elisha Hutchinson, and John Saffin, a committee of the so-called Proprietors of the Narragansett Country, made an agreement with Ezechiel Carré, Peter Le Breton, and other French emigrants, for the settlement of a plantation in the Narragansett Country, to be called Newberry, but subsequently the location was changed on account of its remoteness from the shore, and by another agreement, dated November 4, 1686, the Proprietors or Bay Purchasers agreed to convey to the emigrants a tract in the township of Rochester,* "above yᵉ Long Meadow Kickameeset about Capt John fones his house wherein Each Fam-

* This was the new name given to Kingstown, in June, 1686, by the Government of Dudley, the predecessor of Andros. See Early History of Narragansett, page 106.

ily yt desires it shall have one hundred acres of upland in two Divisions viz A house lott Containing
twenty Acres being twenty Rods broad in ye front
laid out in due ordr wth Street or high way of Six
Rods broad to run between ye sd lotts upon wch they
shall front Secondly yt ye Second division to make
Sd hundred acres of upland shall be laid out on ye
Western Side of ye Sd house lotts as near as ye Land
will bear yt all ye Sd Meadow wth yt wch lieth Adjacent between ye Southern Purchase & a west line
yt is to run from John Androes Northern Corner
above ye Path shall be divided into one hundred
parts each one to have his proportion according to
ye quantity of Land he shall take up & Subscrib for
yt there shall be laid out for ye Sd Mr. Ezechiel Carré
ye pr. sent Minister one hundred and fifty acres of
upland & meadow in ye same manner proportionable
Gratis to him & his heires forevr & one hundred
acres of upland & meadow proportionable to an Or-
thordox Protestant Ministrey & fifty acres of like
land towards the maintainance of a Protestant School
master for ye Town forevr"

The copy of the agreement is signed by Wharton,

Hutchinson, and Saffin, and deeds were to be executed when the terms were complied with.   The names of the French settlers who signed the counterpart were probably the same as those which appear on the plat, viz. :

William Barbret	Grasilier
Paul Collin	Amian
Jean Germon	Lafou
Dechamps	Belhair
Fougere	Milard
Grignon	Jouet
Legaré	Renaud
Robineau	Le gendre
Petter Ayrault	Bertin dit Laronde
Magni Junior	Menardeau
Magni Senior	Galay
Dauid Junior	Ratier
Dauid Senior	Dauid
Chadcno	Beauchamps
foretier	Moize le Brun
Ezechiel Carré, Ministre	Le Breton
Louis Alaire	La Vigne

Jamain	Tauerrier
Bussereau	Bouniot
Le moine	Arnaud
Abraum tourtellot	Lambert
La Veue Galay	Rambert
Targé Junior	Coudret
Targé Senior	Jean Jullien *

It is impossible from the plat to locate the place of
settlement exactly, but the tradition in the Mawney
family and in the neighborhood points to the Mawney
farm and the land around and north of the Briggs
corners, so called, as being the site of it.   On the
northerly part of the Mawney farm in the south-east
corner of East Greenwich, is a place by a spring
which has always been known as the French orchard.
Here are the remains of foundations of cabins or
huts, shell banks, etc., and in my youth there were
the remains of trees said to have been planted by the
French.   Whether this was so or not, the place is
well identified as having always gone by that name,

* In presenting these names, we have faithfully followed the manuscript copy
which has been furnished us from the British State Paper Office, both as to the
division of words or the use of capitals. Errors may possibly have arisen in
transcribing, but they must have occurred before the document reached us.

and the country around it has always been known as
Frenchtown.   The land is now owned by Robert G.
Mawney.

At a place south of the road leading east from the
Briggs corners after crossing the river, are also the
apparent remains of cellars, or foundations of small
houses, where was probably another collection of
dwellings, as they would naturally at first build
their temporary habitations near each other for
mutual assistance and protection.

The highways upon the French plat do not agree
with any highways upon the East Greenwich plat,
which is the one by which the present titles to land
there are held.

Dr. Ayrault, in his memorial, says that the English
ran two highways through his land, and that Thomas
Matteson fenced in a part of it, and Samuel Bennett
and William Weaver built upon it, and from the
position of these names upon the East Greenwich
plat, the probability is that Dr. Ayrault's land was
at the Johnson four corners, next north of the Briggs
corners.

Dr. Ayrault says that the settlement consisted of

forty-five families, and that they soon built twenty-five houses and a church. They had laid out lots for a church and a school and a lot for the minister, Ezechiel Carré. They began to improve their land, then a wilderness of woods and rocks, and seem to have been suffered to remain there without any serious difficulty for several years. When subsequently war broke out between France and England, the French settlers were, by resolution of the General Assembly, of March 3, 1689–90,* allowed to remain unmolested on their taking an oath to comply with the conditions prescribed in the King's Proclamation of War.

In the summer of 1687 the English settlers mowed the grass on the bog meadows, and Governor Andros made an order for the division of it, one-half to the English claimants and the other half to "the French families there, who being strangers and lately settled, and wholly destitute and have no other way to supply themselves."† Dr. Ayrault does not mention this in his memorial.

* R. I. Colonial Records, iii., 264.

† Massachusetts Historical Collections, third series, volume vii., 182. Early History Narragansett, 220.

But about two years after this, more serious troubles began between them and the English inhabitants, which led to the breaking up of the settlement and the removal of nearly all. Dr. Ayrault states that two families removed to Boston and the rest to New York, but it is well-known that the Le moines (Mawneys) and Targés (Tourgees) remained there, and Dr. Ayrault himself remained in East Greenwich for several years afterwards and finally removed to Newport, and was one of the first promoters of the foundation of the Episcopal Church there.*

To a person unacquainted with Rhode Island history, it may seem strange that any dissension should arise between the English settlers, many of whom had been driven from Massachusetts on account of their religion, and a number of French settlers who had been obliged to leave their country for the same cause. They were alike, protestants, and all contending for the largest liberty of conscience.

But there were land speculators and rings in those days as well as now, and then as now some of the leaders stood high in the church.

*See Arnold's Rhode Island, volume i., Appendix G.

The charter of Rhode Island of 1663 had secured to Rhode Island certain limits. But for all the outer borders of their territory they had for many years to contend with Connecticut and Massachusetts. It was not until 1746 that Rhode Island gained possession of the eastern portion of their charter grant; the western portion, and especially the Narragansett country, was the subject of continual conflict; Rhode Island did not acquire peaceable possession of it until 1707; the boundary was not actually settled until the decision of the King in council in 1728.

This conflict of jurisdiction gave rise to great confusion in claims to lands.

In June and July, 1659, Major Humphrey Atherton and his associates, afterwards known, sometimes as the Atherton company, and again as the Bay Purchasers, purchased from the Indian sachems two large tracts of land, Quidneset and Boston Neck. These were called the northern and southern purchases. They included some of the most valuable lands in the west part of the Colony, both from quality of soil and from their advantageous situation, on Narragansett Bay.

This company consisted at first of Major Humphrey Atherton, of Massachusetts, John Winthrop, Governor of Connecticut, Richard Smith, Sen., and R. Smith, Jr., of Wickford, William Hudson and Amos Richardson, of Boston, and John Tinker, of Nashaway.* Major Atherton had been employed by Massachusetts in negotiating with the Indians, and having been for several years superintendent of the *praying* Indians, he had thus acquired an influence with them. They made offers of land to Roger Williams to induce him to become one of the company, but he refused and informed them that their purchases were illegal.† It will be seen that the company was so formed as to combine different influences, and included besides persons from Massachusetts and Connecticut, some from Rhode Island.

Subsequently Wharton, Saffin, Edward Hutchinson, and others, became interested in the purchases.‡

But the trouble about the Frenchtown lands grew out of another transaction. The Commissioners of

* Potter's Early History of Narragansett, 209, 58.

† Roger Williams's Letter to Major Mason. See Early History of Narragansett, page 102.

‡ Early History of Narragansett, 209, etc.

the United Colonies had undertaken to impose a fine
upon the Indians in the jurisdiction claimed by
Rhode Island, and on non-payment, had sent a mili-
tary force and compelled the Narragansett sachems
to execute a mortgage, September 29, 1680, of their
whole country to them.* The Indians not paying
the fine, the Atherton company paid it for them, and
the sachems made a new mortgage of the whole
country to the company, conditioned to pay the
money in six months. On the expiration of that
time two sachems, with some other Indians, in September, 1662, delivered formal possession by turf
and twig, to the Atherton partners. How much the
Indians knew of the effect of these proceedings may
be imagined. It was nothing but a mere farce.

The Rhode Island Legislature afterwards, in 1672,
confirmed the Boston Neck and Quidneset purchases,† but they never acknowledged the validity of
this mortgage. If these lands were within the limits
of the Rhode Island charter, as they were afterwards
decided to be, then all these proceedings were wholly

* Early History of Narragansett, 60, 234.
† Early History of Narragansett, 214, 77.

void.   The Atherton claim had been rejected by Governor Andros, and the Atherton company had petitioned the English government for a grant of land to include the land they had sold to the French. But it does not appear that they ever obtained it.*

It was under their claim to hold the Narragansett country by this mortgage, that the Atherton company had made the grant to the French settlers in 1686.

Nine years before this time, in October, 1677, the Legislature of Rhode Island had made a grant of this territory and established a township, then and still known as East Greenwich,† and it was platted out to the settlers.‡

These facts are sufficient to enable us to account for the subsequent troubles.

On the 22d of April, 1700, we learn from the Colo-

* Arnold's Rhode Island, i., 505, 507.

† A resolution of the Rhode Island Legislature to establish the Greenwich settlement had been passed at an earlier date, but in October, 1677, a special grant of the township was made to certain persons by name. Peleg Sanford and Benjamin Speere were appointed to survey it. John Smith, of Newport, was afterwards appointed in place of Speere. In 1700, the original plat being lost, a copy was proved and established by the General Assembly. The plat now in existence bears date 1716, and was made by William Hall, surveyor. R. I. Col. Rec., vol. ii., 574; and vol. iii., 7, 26, 51, 403.

‡ Potter's Early History of Narragansett, pp. 110, 111.

nial Records* that a court of enquiry had been held in Kingstown to enquire into a riot there, and that Dr. Ayrault's son Daniel and several Englishmen were fined for participation in it. The General Assembly afterwards set aside a part of the proceedings as illegal. But Dr. Ayrault was tried before the General Court of Tryals at Newport, September 3, 1700, for nuisance and was ordered to open the highways, meaning of course the highways as laid out by the English settlers. Dr. Ayrault says, that they opened the highways through his land in two directions. This fact seems to aid us in identifying the Johnson four-corners, as the location of the land he occupied.

In 1687, a French protestant visited New England, and examined the country with a view to ascertain and report upon its advantages for settlement. Some of his letters were published for the first time in the Bulletin Historique of the Societé de l'Histoire du Protestantisme Francais, in February, 1867. They were translated by E. T. Fisher, and published in the Liberal Christian, a newspaper

* R. I. Col. Rec., iii., 413. Potter's Early History of Narragansett, 109.

published in New York, and since re-published in a quarto pamphlet, at Brooklyn, New York, in 1868, under the title of "Report of a French Protestant Refugee in Boston, 1687."

He made a visit to the French settlement in Rhode Island, but unfortunately the letter written in December, 1687, in which he gave an account of it is lost. In another letter, November, 1687, he briefly mentions it thus : "There are at Narragansett about one hundred persons of the faith. M. Carré* is their minister."

This is all the information we can obtain in regard to the settlement. Several families remained in Rhode Island without being disturbed : two families at least in the very neighborhood where the strife occurred : thus showing that the trouble did not grow out of their nationality. In a subsequent part

---

* A sermon by M. Carré was printed at Boston in 1689, under the following title, "The charitable Samatarian, a sermon on the tenth chapter of Luke, verses 30-35. Pronounced in the French Church at Boston, by Ezechiel Carré, formerly Minister of Rochechalais, (sic) in France, now Minister of the French Colony on Narraganset, translated into English, by N. Walter." This title is taken from the Brinley Catalogue. The little volume found its way from the Brinley sale to the Library of Congress.

of this memoir, we shall give some account of several of the families of the Frenchtown settlement, and of some other French settlers in Rhode Island.

It is with great difficulty that their descendants can now be traced, so great have been the changes and corruptions of the names. Two or three such have already been noted, for instance, Le Moine became Money and still later Mawney; Ganeaux became Gano; Daillé became Daily or Daly; Targé became Tourgee. Many others might be shown but these suffice to explain the difficulty in following them. Upon the breaking up of the Narragansett settlement, many of the settlers went to the southern states. Among those who probably thus again emigrated were Pierre Collin, Daniel Jouet, Moyez Le Brun, Daniel Le Gendre, Louis de St. Julien, and Legree.

DOCUMENTS

RELATING TO THE

FRENCH SETTLEMENTS

IN THE

COLONY OF RHODE ISLAND,

FROM THE

BRITISH STATE PAPER OFFICE, LONDON.

THE CONTRACT WITH THE BAY PURCHASERS.

Whereas there was Articles of Agreement made & Concluded Between Richd Wharton Esqr Elisha Hutchinson & John Saffin ye Committee for ye propriet^{rs} of ye Narragans^{tt} Country & Ezekiell Carré Peter Berton & oth^{rs} french Gentlemen their friends & Associates whose names are thereunto Subscribed Bearing date ye 12th day of Octo^r last Concerning ye Settlem^t of a Place called Newberry Plantations in ye Narragans^{tt} Country wch upon Second Consideration in regard of ye Remoateness of ye same from ye Sea they have by ye Mutual Consent of ye S^d Committee declined ye Settlement of ye S^d Plantation & ye S^d Master Ezekiell Carré Master Berton in behalfe of themselves & oth^{rs} their friends & Associates who have hereunto Subscribed are now Come to & have made a new Agreem^t In manner & forme

following this 4th day of Nouembr 1686 Annoqr
R R S Jacobi Secundi Anglia & Secundo Viz
    Imprimus That ye Sd Richd Wharton Esqr Capt
Elisha Hutchinson & John Saffin ye aforesd Committee do by these Prsents Couenant Grant & Agree to
& wth ye Sd Ezekiell Carré Peter Berton French
Gentlemen their friends & Associates who have hereunto Subscribed to lay out A meet & Considerable
tract of Land in ye Township of Rochester* above
ye Long Meadow Kickameeset about Capt John fones
his house wherein Each Family yt desires it shall
have one hundred Acres of upland in two Divisions
viz A house lott Containing twenty Acres being
twenty Rods broad in ye front laid out in due ordr
wth Street or high way of Six Rode broad to run
between ye Sd lotts upon wch they shall front Secondly yt ye Second devission to make ye Sd hundred
acres of upland shall be laid out on ye Western Side
of ye Sd house lotts as near as ye Land will bear
yt all ye Sd Meadow wth yt wch lieth Adjacent between ye Southern Purchase and a west line yt is to
run from John Androes Northern Corner above
ye Path shall be divided into one hundred parts each

* See note page 13.

one to have his proportion according to ye quantity
of Land he shall take up & Subscrib for y^t there
shall be laid out for ye S^d Mr Ezekiel Carré y^e
p^rsent Minister one hundred & fifty acres of upland
& meadow in ye same manner proportionable Gratis
to him & his heires forev^r & one hundred acres of
upland & meadow proportionable to an Orthodox
Protestant Ministrey & fifty acres of like land towards
the Maintainance of a Protestant Schoolmaster for
ye Town forev^r y^t for Every hundred Acres of Land
be it upland or meadow laid out in forme aforeS^d
each one shall pay pay unto ye S^d Comittee or Assignes twenty pounds in Currant money or in goods
answ^{r}able to their Satisfaction y^t those y^t are not
able to do or se cause at p^rsent to pay for their Land
they shall have three years time for payment at
ye rate of twenty five pounds per hundred acres laid
out as aforeS^d & So According to Proportion for
w^t Land they shall take up & Subscribe for & in
Case they doe not pay w^{th}in the tearme of three
years each one Shall pay Interest for ye Same at
ye rate of Six per cent & for w^t money any one shall
pay sooner it shall be abated accordingly y^t untill

yᵉ Sᵈ Meadow be divided those yᵗ inhabit first on
yᵉ place in AforeSᵈ Shall have the Benefitt of Im-
provemᵗ & likewise of yᵉ undivided Lands Adjacent
untill they be othʳwise disposed yᵗ upon payment
of yᵉ money for yᵉ Land as aforeSᵈ & Leagall Deeds
shall be Given Signed & Sealed by yᵉ Sᵈ Committee
to Each one According to his Proportion of Land
Granted In Wittness whereof the Parties within mentioned have each for themselves Interchangable Sett
their hands & Seales the day and year above written

 Signed Sealed & Delivered

by Mr Hutchinson & Saffin Richard Wharton (·)

 In the presence of Elisha Hutchinson (·)

Walter Steuen Junʳ   John Saffin (·)

Lodowick Updick

John Gore

Alexander Huling A true Coppy Extracted out

      of yᵉ Originall & Compaired

      Octoʳ yᵉ 13ᵗʰ in yᵉ year 1692

    By me John Heath Conservatʳ

[Indorsed] Coppy of Mr Wharton &c agreemᵗ with
Ezekiell Carré &c for Settleing a town in the Narra-
gansᵗ

THE COMPLAINT AND REMONSTRANCE

DR. AYRAULT.

———◆———

The Complaint & Remonstrance of Petter Ayrault
In Habitant in ye French Town in Narragans^tt of
Some Iregularities & Inhumanities Proceed upon him
July 23th 1700 by Some of ye Inhabitants of y^e
Town of East Greenwick in Said Narragans^tt Viz^t
That upon ye 23th of S^d July, there Came unto
my house in S^d French Town aft^r Sun Sett a great
number of ye town of Greenwick mixt wth some of
Warrwick & Chantecutt who told me y^t ye Court on
ye oth^r side ye River wch was keept at ye house of
Pardon Tillinghast in S^d Town desired to speak w^th
me I told them I was unwilling to go, out of my
house so late at night who Replyed we have a Warrant & if you will not go fairly we will force you.

Upon wch I asked them for a Sight of their warrant
& to Read ye same to me wch ye Utterly Refused &
putt ye same in their Pocketts notwthstanding I was
very Importunate wth them to give me a Coppy of
their Warrant for my mony wch they absolutely Refused & Instantly laid their hands upon me & dragged
me to ye River Side & aft^rwards ov^r s^d river & placed
me in their Court as they Called it at y^t time of
Night where I was Interrogeted by them or most of
them of S^d Court my Reply to them was I was a
Stranger & Und^rstood not English & therefore desired I might have an Interpreter they told me I
should have one, on ye Morrow Soe they left me &
my Son Dan^{ll} at liberty upon Sam^{ll} Bennetts word
y^t I would answer it Next day wch accordingly I did
& Gave bond for my appearance to the next Court
lett it be Consid^{red} y^t I was Sett upon In my own
house at y^t Unseasonable time wth a Warrant w^{ch}
they were ashamed to read or give a Coppy of In
fine my wife an aged Woman of Sixty years of Age
Infirm & Sick Could not by all her Cryes & Teares
perswade them to Disiste but Contraywise did Strike
& flung hir on ye Pavement.-where she Continued

Some time for dead all wch I Conceive is not only UnNaturall & Inhumaine & against all Law & Reason wch I Submit to a further Determination

Pierre Ayrault

Aug^{sst} 5th 1700

Allso ye Most Notorious & Ill behaviour of Sam^{ll} Davis & Abner Spencer to my Son Daniell Ayrault who they found at my house ye Same time I was fetcht away & wthout cause for ye same they tooke my S^d Son & Puling him out of my house took by the head Feet carried him along some Part of the way to said Tillinghast spoken of & flinging down on the Stones Pulling him a long Giving him no reason for their so doing and bringing him before their Court so called lett him goe whose Complaint of Injustice to them no notice was taken of, thus are we endangered of being ruened & Destroyed by Such lawles persons So I have great cause to seek releiff therein

Pierre Ayrault

August: 5: 1700.

Newport August: 7: 1700 Doctor Pierre Ayrault appeared before us whose names are here Under written whose are Commissionated to hear & Enquire into y^e Irregularityes Cmomitted in y^e Colony of Rhode Island & Provid^ce Plantations & S^d Ayrault haveing made his Complaint of Injustice done him and haveing on the other Leafe Given it Under his hand did upon his Corporall Oath before us aver it to be y^e Reall Truth.

> Francis Brinley $\left.\right\}$ Commissio^rs
> Peleg Sanford
> Nath Coddington

[Indorsed.] true Coppy of Perre Ayrault Complaint of abuse receiv^d

July 23: 1700.

FURTHER COMPLANT AND REMONSTRANCE

OF

DR. AYRAULT.

———◆———

May it Please yor Excellency

I Lately made bold to Lay before yor Excellency by Petition Some part of my grivances & wrongs done me on my lands purchased in ye Narragans^{tt} Country in ye Town of Rochester of ye proprie^{rs} thereof & have here given a short and true Remonstrance of myself & Distressed Country people Settlem^t & ye sever^{ll} Occurances and Passages they & myself past thro there

Upon the fourth day of Nouemb^r 1686 Richard Wharton Esqr &c & on our part our Minist^r Ezekiel Carré & Peter Berton agrees for a Sertain parsell of Land in S^d Narragans^{tt} Country for Settling A Town thereon of an hundred acres apiece to a family w^{ch}

was done & Compleated o^r sever^{ll} allotments laid out
& a Coppy of ye Articles I make bold to p^rsent
yor Excellency wth, & wth a true Coppy of ye Platt
of o^r sever^{ll} Settlem^t & Allotment as Laid out &
we was there Settled by ye then Proprie^{rs} & Gov-
erm^t who gaue us ye oath of Alleagance we being
about forty five five familys building about twenty five
houses wth Some Sellars in ye Ground Setting up
o^r Church & it being a very wilderness Country fild
alltogether wth wood & stones & no former Improvements made thereon y^t o^r Labour charge & trouble
was great but we had A Comfort we could then Injoy
o^r worship to God & had ye Goverm^{ts} Protection to
us in o^r Improvem^{ts} no p^rson disturbing us on our
Labour no P^rtending any claime to any of ye soile
but they purchases of S^d Lands by whom we were
Setled we paying all takes to the Goverment as was
laid on us we peaceable Injoyed our Lands & Im-
provements wthout any thing of y^e least molestation
Under the then Goverment

   The then Goverm^t being Removed we was then
taken Und^r y^e Goverm^t of y^e Colony of Rhode
Island &c who seemed to treat us civelly also at y^e

first not Molesting us & upon y^e 20 of February
$16\frac{88}{90}$ they Gener^{ll} Court past an Act y^t we should
be Sent for to Warwick by Maj^r John Green one of
the Assis^{ts} whereby it should be signified unto us his
Maj^{ties} Pleasure of an Act of Indulgance unto such
frenchmen as we, y^t we Should be required to take
y^e Oath of Alleigance to his then p^{r}sent Maj^{ty} w^{ch}
according to S^d Gen^{ll} Court Act we were sent for
to Warwick & Gave o^r oath of Alleigance & had his
Maj^{ties} Act of Indulgence read to us & a Promise of
our Protection from S^d Goverm^t Und^r o^r Libertys &
Propertys

But the obseruance of S^d Act of Indulgence & y^e
Protecting of us in o^r libertys & Propertys wee continued not two years Und^r S^d Goverm^t before we
were molested by ye Uulgar Sort of they People who
flynging down of o^r fences laying open our Lands to
ruen Soe that all Benefitt thereby we were Deprived
thereof (ruen looked on us in a Dismall State o^r
wives & children liveing in fear of ye threats of
many unruly p^{r}sons) & w^t Benefit we Expected
from o^r Lands for Subsistance was destroyed by
Secretly Laying open o^r fences by night & day &

w^t little we had p^{r}serued by flying from france we
had laid out und^r ye then Improvements looked so
hard upon us to see ye Cryes of o^r wives & Children
Lamenting their sad fate flying from Persecution and
Comeing Under his Majesties Gracious Indulgance
And by ye Goverm^t promised us yet we Ruened &
when we Complained to the Goverm^t we could have
no relief altho some would a helped us we Judge If
by their Patience they could a Born Such Ill Treat-
ments as they must expect to a meet wth by ye Unruly Inhabitants their Settled also many of ye English Inhabitants Compassionating o^r Condition would
a helped us but when they used any means therein
they were Evilly treated so y^t these things did put
us then upon looking for a place of Shelter in o^r Diss-
tresed Condition & hereing y^t many of o^r Distressed
Country people had been protected & well treated in
Boston & Yorke some of o^r principale persons went
to Boston & York to seek out new Habitations where
ye Goverm^{tts} had Compassion of them & gave them
relief, & help to their wives & Children Subsistance
only two familys moveing to Boston & they rest to
New York & their bought Lands some of them & had

time given them for payment & so was they all
forced away from their Lands & houses orchards &
vineyards taking some small matter from some English people for somew^t of their Labour thus Leave-
ing all habitations some people got not anything for
their Labour & Improvem^ts but Greenwich men who
had given us ye disturbance giting on ye Land so
Improved in any way they Could & soon demolished
& puld down o^r Church

But I being perswaded by many to stay & haveing
fenced in fifty Acres of Land purchased & made very
good Improvements by a large Orchard Garden &
Uineyard & a good house was willing to keep my
Settlement & bear all outrages Comitted Against me
wch furth^r shall be related to, and as many p^rsons
who in their Sickness and Extremity would send for
me to Administer help unto them wch Under God's
Goodness I have been a help to raise many from
Extream Sickness yet have they soon forgot my
Labour & rewarded me wth Endeavours to root me
out of my habitations & by flynging down my fences
y^t I might not have any Subsistance by my Land
these Endeavo^rs not succeeding in all their Endeavours and oth^r Contrivance was against me

Upon the 25 of Jan^r $16\frac{9.5}{6}$ one Giles Pearse &
John Smith agreed togeath^r in a Clandistine manner
to gitt me out of my habitation & Improvem^{ts} & for
y^t end S^d Pearse sells one part of my Land about
twenty five Acres to S^d Smith in S^d Deed Containing
my houses orchards Gardens & most part of y^e best
of my Improved Lands & in S^d Deed was allso Comprehended ye habitations to houses & Lands of three
oth^r persons then Liveing on S^d Lands this being
about tenn years after o^r Settlements & Improvem^{ts}
as mentioned S^d deed takeing in Ninety Acres of
Lands (as mentioned all wthin fences & Improvements) & ye same day ye deed was Signed & Sealed
& ye witnesses spoken to not to Deuvlge their
secreed act the same day they went to Greenwich both
Smith & Pearse before a Justice of ye Peace one
John Heath & acknowledged it to be their act before
S^d Justice & ye 27th day of S^d month S^d Justice of
ye Peace who had ye records of Greenwich placed
S^d deed on record & S^d Justice herein was privy &
Knowing to ye S^d Clandistine Acts of S^d Pearse &
Smith who certainly knew ye sale of ye Land Und^r
w^t Circumstances ye were und^r After this S^d Smith

& Adherance gave me much trouble & ye rest of us puling down o^r fences & I Complained to ye Authority neuer could find relief I Keeping my house y^t ye Could not have any Opportunity to Enter in (to dispossess me & these Actiones not takeing Effect for in my distress many of Neighbours did Comfort me) y^t their would be some relief from ye Crown to me & they Proprie^{rs} of S^d Country & then anoth^r projecct was put in Execution against me for as I have declared Greenwich men at their pleasure Extended their lines* time aft^r time without any authority as I Understand from y^e Propriet^{rs} of S^d Country or y^e Gen^{ll} Court & took in at last all y^e French Town & upon y^e 14th of febr $\frac{1699}{1700}$ Greenwich & Sever^{ll} of y^e Town of Warwick wth a Plat of such a parsell of land wch they Called Greenwich Township p^{r}sents it to y^e Gener^{ll} Assembly y^e Assembly Confirms y^e Lands comprehended in S^d Plat to be w^{thin} Green-

---

* Dr. Ayrault complains that the English kept encroaching on them. He does not seem to have had the least knowledge that there was a dispute as to the title to the lands. So far from encroaching on them, there is not the least evidence that the bounds of the grant made to the English settlers by the Colony of Rhode Island were ever changed in that neighborhood. Farther east they were changed, and the State Records give the particulars.

wich Township wthout Consid^{r}ing y^t Greenwich had
Intrenched upon ye oth^r towns adjoyning & they
haveing ye Jurisdiction soon set to work for my
Ruen in anoth^r way in w^t ye Could

And as I have now S^d & given an accou^{tt} of my
Settlem^t fenceing & Improvements & so about four-
teen years aft^r upon ye 23 of July 1700 two of y^e
Assist^s of Warwick (viz) Benjn Barton & Benjn
Smith came to ye new Township of Greenwich w^{ch}
had Swallowed up all ye french Town bringing wth
them a number of Warwick & Greenwich men & at
ye house of one Pardon Tillinghast one of ye houses
in ye french Town there they held a Court of Enquiry as they called it one Capt John Fones wth
Sever^{ll} oth^{rs} hereing of S^d Appointed Court came
to Inspect into their Proceedings & Capt John Fones
took an acco^{tt} thereof, of y^t days Proceedall whilest
he was their wth his oath given to ye same a true
Coppy Thereof I have allso here laid before yor
Excellency also a true Coppy how I was dealt wth
y^t Evening aft^r Sun Down how there came to my
house a great Numb^r of Greenwich & Warwick people & wthout shewing me any warrant for w^t they

Came for draging me Away to their Court house &
ye result of ye Court ye next day & how by their
Plat obtained by ye Assembly in ye month of February 1699 before past they sett out two highways to
run through my Land & bound me in a bond to the
next Court wch by ye Gov^rs Warrant & oth^rs Signing
wth him afterwards was laid out one of S^d highways
on one Side of my Land ye whole Length thereof
Runing through my orchard ten Rod in wideth de-
stroying my orchard part of wch Land one Thos
Mattison have since fenced in & Improves & y^e
oth^r highway they ord^red to run athirt my Land
takeing away above twenty acres of my Land y^e
wch one Sam^ll Bennett & Wm Weaver have built
thereon & Improves S^d Land so y^t of my fifty Acres
I haue about twenty Acres left me & y^e (known
highway) or Road into ye Country y^t allways was &
lay on ye oth^r Side of my S^d Land since S^d Action
ye Widow Smith widow of ye S^d John Smith herein
mentioned have fenced in every part thereof setting
a house on Part of S^d highway & no notice taken
thereof thus I can but in a Brief give yor Excellency
a short Acco^tt of Part of my trouble & Pray all En-

deavours may be used to give Relief to your Distressed & most Humble Seruant

                                    Pierre Ayrault

Greenwich August 20 : 1705.

[Indorsed.] Doctor Ayrault remonstrance of his Troubles.

PROCEEDINGS OF THE COURT

FRENCHTOWN, JULY 23, 1700.

———◆———

Narrag : st   Att a Court held at ye House of Pardon Tillinghast att ye French Town or Plantation so called in Kings Province July 23 1700.

Present.

Mr Benjn Barton Assist
Mr Benjn Smith Assist
Mr John Spencer Justice
Mr John Heath Clerke
Mr Thomas Fry Attorney
   The Jury returned but not by the Sheriff (viz)
Mr Peter Greene Foreman
Mr Benjn Greene
Mr Jabesh Greene
Mr Amos Stafford

Mr Jeremiah Westcot

Mr Othenell Gorton

Mr Sam^{ll} Gorton Junr

Mr Charles Holdon

Mr Joseph Stafford

Mr John Potter

Mr John Burton

Mr Thos Burlingham

The Court being Sate ye Jury was called to take their Engagements which was Administred unto them (but not According to Form of ye Oath nor Engagement to a Grand Enquest) wherein they were charged in Behalfe of o^r Soueraigne Lord the King to Enquire into ye High way's y^t were Stopped & Fenced in but not Nameing ye Town & to make a returne to y^t Court then Mr Attorney Placeing him-selfe at ye Upper End of ye Table at ye right hand of ye Justices & Pulled out some papers & Desired ye Justices & Jury to take Notice of w^t he had to Lay before them then caused an Act of an Assembly to be read by ye Clarke wherein was granted 5000 Acres of Land to be Laid out in ye Narraganset Country for ye Settling of an Town & This 5000

Acres Should be divided amongst Fifty persons whom ye S^d Assembly did See cause to accommodate therew^th to be to them & their heirs & Assignes for evr: Provided they did observe ye Prescriptions & Injunctions y^t was laid upon them by ye S^d Grant & perform ye same accordingly or oth^rways to forfiet ye S^d lands Granted then was read an Ord^r for ye Laying out ye Lands & Shewed a paper wch they called a Platforme of those Lands laid out by themselves w^thout form & w^thout Scale or Compass or ye Suruayers Name to it or mens to ye divisions Laid out or anything of Sertainty in it for finding out ye highway but according to w^t those wch were ye Evidences given into ye Jury wch they doe Say & Aver to ye wch p^rsons at y^t time may be Known to be very Young & at y^t time not Capable to Know ye bounds nor Concernes of Each Divisions as ye lines or bounds then were or where ye highways were then ye S^d Attorney read An Ord^r of their Town where himself was by them Constituted & Appointed to be their Attorney & it their behalf to Plead in any of his Maj^ties Courts of Judicature in defence of their rights & Priviledges then he read a Coppy of a

Letter he had Sent unto ye Govr declareing their
pretended agrieuances as y^t there high ways was
stopped & fenced in by some p^{r}sons & desired their
might be a Court of Enquiry & a Jury to find out
ye highways & make returne thereof & then he read
ye Gover^{rs} Answer to him y^t it should be done
accordingly then he pleaded ye Lands & highways
was laid out According to Ord^r & were recorded in
their Booke of records & y^t there were Evidences
y^t would Shew unto ye Jury where ye highways
were but I did not see those Evidences Sworne in
ye Face of ye Court So ye Jury was sent forth &
some of Greenwich men went wth them then ye Court
rise Up abruptly & disapated Untill their Dinner was
Sett ready for them then ye Jury was sent for to go
to Dinner wth them before they had agreed Upon A
Verdict Aft^r Dinner some private Consultation wth
ye Jury they went out again & staid out till Allmost
night only I did obserue y^t two p^{r}sons of S^d Jury
did come to advise wth ye Justices Privately in y^e
S^d house & Aft^{r}wards returned to their Fellows &
neer night as before S^d came & delivered their verdict wch was as neer as I can remember in these

words Following (viz) Wee the Jury Inquiry for o[r]
Soueraigne Lord y[e] King doe find y[t] Docter Peter
Auralt hath Presumptiously fenced in y[e] highway
according to Evidences Given to us & therefore
Guilty y[e] w[ch] S[d] Verdict y[e] Court did accept then
did I myself make a request unto y[e] S[d] Court to
Grant Mee A Coppy of S[d] Verdict w[ch] I did in behalfe of Doct[r] Peter Auralt He being y[e] Object as I
did und[r]stand they Pitched upon according to S[d] Verdict but could not obtain it Neither was y[e] S[d] Doct[r]
called for to here y[e] Play made against him nor y[e]
Evidences given in Unto y[e] Jury nor their Verdict
when Delivered then y[e] Court rise up again abruptly
& went into y[e] house to Confer about some private
Matt[rs] w[ch] they did Intend to Effect w[ch] I was not
aware of Neith[r] did I think or Imagine any thing of
w[t] they Intended w[ch] aft[r] my Departure they put
in Practice as I am Informed but seeing y[e] sun was
neer Upon Setting & those of my Company being
desirous to returne home I went into y[e] house where
y[e] S[d] Justices were & took my Leave of them w[ch]
as I do Conjecture they were glad to here of my departure they sent for S[d] Doct[r] Peter Auralt who

Early ye next Morning came to my house & gave me
an acco^tt of their Injurious Actions against him his
son & wife wch their may be sever^ll Evidences y^t can
testify to ye Truth therefore

Declared and Attested
per John Fones

Newport August : 8 : 1700

Capt John Fones Came before us whose Names
are Under Written and Upon his Corporall Oath did
declare that ye w^thin written paper to wch he hath
sett his hand unto is ye truth And nothing but y^e
truth Taken as Abovesaid

> Francis Brinley
> Peleg Sanford   } Commissio^rs
> Nathl Coddington

[Indorsed] Capt Fones Euidence about Doct^r Perre
Ayrault

MASSACHUSETTS BAY PROPRIETORS.

———◆———

THE constant attempt of the authorities of Massachusetts to interfere in the affairs of Rhode Island, and to subjugate the Indians and the chartered territory of the Rhode Island Colony to her jurisdiction, deserve more than a passing notice, as they were the cause not only of the troubles with the French emigrants, but of most of the early troubles and sufferings of our ancestors. We should have had no Indian wars with their attendant massacres, but for their meddling interference.

Their attempts to convert the Indians to Massachusetts Christianity, were not looked upon with favor by the Rhode Island authorities. These attempts were no doubt considered here as a part of a

scheme to gain favor with the Indians and establish
authority over Narragansett. Roger Williams made
many efforts to Christianize the natives, but with
little success. In one of his letters dated 1654, he
says: "At my last departure for England, I was
importuned by the Narragansett Sachems and especially by Ninigret, to present their petition to the
High Sachems of England, that they might not be
forced from their religion, and for not changing their
religion to be invaded by war. For they said they
were daily visited by Indians that came from the
Massachusetts, that if they would not pray, they
should be destroyed by war."[1] Ninigret, on being
requested by Mayhew, to give him leave to preach
to his people, bade him go and make the English
good first. They said it was too difficult for them
to understand.[2] The conduct of Christian nations
and people, was then as now, the greatest obstacle to
the spread of Christianity.

The ill feeling of the religious people of Massachusetts towards the heretics of Rhode Island, was
manifested in various ways. When Rhode Island

1. Potter's Early History Narragansett, 122, 154, 155.
2. Neal's New England, London, 1740, v. 1, p. 275.

for her own protection applied to be admitted into the Confederation of the Colonies, she was repulsed. The refusal of the authorities of Massachusetts to sell powder to the people of Rhode Island, is but one example of the prevailing spirit.[1] This may have been done under a pretence of a general law.[2]

They invaded the territory of Rhode Island at pleasure, and made constant attempts to get the Rhode Island Indians to submit to them. The Rhode Islanders and Indians were generally on good terms. The great Indian war of 1676, was considered by the people of Rhode Island, as brought on by the misconduct of the English themselves.[3] The great Sachem Miantinomo had been put to death by the direction of the Massachusetts authorities, and under the advice of the elders of the church.[4] And the editor of Winthrop is obliged to express his con-

1. Coit's History of Puritanism, pp. 295, 524. Benedict's History of the Baptists, ed. of 1813, v. 1, p. 466. Arnold's History of Rhode Island, v. 1, pp. 158, 258. R. I. Col. Rec., v. 1, p. 324; letter of Roger Williams.

2. Ancient Charters and Laws of Massachusetts Bay, p. 133, dates in margin 1633, 1637.

3. Potter's Early History Narragansett, p. 93; also R. I. Hist. Col., (Callender,) v. 4, p. 126, in note.

4. Winthrop's History of New England, ed. of 1826, v. 2, p. 131.

demnation of it.   These wars against the Indians were conducted with a savageness not surpassed in more recent times.   Their prisoners who were not butchered were sold into slavery to the Bermuda, or West India Islands.[1]

The Puritans of Massachusetts, the term is used to denote the dominant clergy who governed the colony without regard to mere minor differences of opinion, have been held up to the world as a set of saints for whom this world was not good enough. Let us see.

They professed to be driven over here for the sake of religious liberty.   No such thing.   They had that in Holland.   But there they could not lord it over others.   They could not punish heresy in their flock.   And they were afraid of being gradually scattered or swallowed up by their Dutch neighbors. They came over, as most emigrants go to new countries, to better their condition, and they did it. Never did any set of men know better how to reconcile Godliness and land grabbing than they did.

1. Coit's History of Puritanism, p. 411. Potter's Early Hist. Narragansett, 28, 80, 83, 84, 94.

And as for religious freedom, they never allowed it. Mrs. Hemans' five verses can be enjoyed by those who can substitute their imagination for facts, but when she says,

> " They left unstained what there they found
> Freedom to worship God,"

a greater falsehood was never put into poetry, and if we enjoy religious liberty at the present day, we owe no thanks to the Puritans of Massachusetts for it.

For all the outrages and abominations practiced by the Massachusetts government towards the Indians and Rhode Islanders, the Puritan clergy must be held responsible.   The clergy were supreme in the state.   No one but a church member could vote, or be a magistrate or juror.   This of course gave the clergy complete control.[1]   As a matter of course, all the politicians and office holders were very pious and very orthodox.   If General Butler had been a candidate for governor in those days, he would have been obliged to play the rôle of a saint with cropped

---

1. As to the effect of this, see Savage's Winthrop new ed. of 1853, vol. 2, 171, 200.

hair, white bands and sanctimonious visage and
looked like some of those old ministers whose
pictures, for want of something better, used to be
hung up over the doors and in the recesses of the
old Harvard College library. And he would have
gained in popularity by hanging a few Quakers
and witches. Everything was done under the advice
of the ministers. When the great Sachem Miantonomo was treacherously taken prisoner in a war
between him and other Indian tribes, they advised
his death, and are responsible for the savage manner of its execution, and thus in a great measure
for the subsequent wars and massacres. When they
marched into Rhode Island to carry out the great
Indian butchery of 1676, the first of their "Laws and
ordinances of war," provided that no man should
blaspheme the Trinity, on pain of having his tongue
" bored with a hot iron."

The Puritan clergy thus taking the lead in politics
and in war, the Puritan soldiery butchered the Indians in most approved modern style. And in
treachery they exceeded the moderns of the West.
One hundred and twenty Indians surrendered to

Captain Eels on a pledge of protection. The government, disregarding the pledge, carried them to Plymouth, and sold and transported them all into slavery. And the descendants of those men are probably now slaves in the West India Islands, perhaps in Cuba.[1] When the Indian Sachem Canonchet was taken, in order to give the Indian allies a share in the barbarities, and thus attach them to the whites, "by the prudent advice of the English commanders," the Pequods shot him, Mohicans cut off his head and quartered him, Ninigret's men burned the quarters, and his head was sent to the council at Hartford.[2]

When King Philip was taken, he was quartered,[3] and the pieces hung on four trees. His head and hands were carried first to Rhode Island. The Puritans proclaimed a thanksgiving on the 17th of August, and on that day his head was carried in triumph into Plymouth, and after being exhibited through the

1. Potter's Early Hist. Narragansett, 80. Church's Indian War, Drake's ed., 1829, p. 52. Morton's Memorial, Davis's ed., 1826, p. 443.

2. Potter's Early Hist. Narragansett, p. 96. Hubbard's Indian Wars, 1803, p. 168. Baylies' Hist. Plymouth, pt. 3, p. 117.

3. Church's Indian War, Drake's ed., 1829, p. 125.

country, was exposed on a gibbet where it remained
for thirty years.[1]   The prayers of Church, to save the
life of Annawon were disregarded, and he was be-
headed.   Tispaquin, another chief, surrendered on
a pledge of protection from Church,[2] and he was
executed with Annawon, "a dastardly act," says
Baylies, "which disgraced the government," who
thereby basely "violated the English faith."[3]   When
Philip's son, a boy of nine years of age, was taken
prisoner, his case was referred to the clergy for
advice.   John Cotton and Samuel Arnold were for
putting him to death, quoting texts of Scripture
to sustain their opinions; others were more merciful,
and he was sold as a slave and shipped to Bermuda.[4]
In the Pequot war the male Indian children were
sold to Bermuda, the women and female children
were scattered about among the towns.[5]   Some of

1. Baylies' Hist. Plymouth, pt. 3, 452.   Drake's Ed. of Hubbard, v. 1, p. 272.

2. As to Church's authority to promise protection, see Baylies' Hist. Plymouth, pp. 3, 150;   also Church's Indian War, Drake's ed., 1829, p. 96.

3. Baylies' Hist. Plymouth, pt. 3, 183, 184.   Church's Indian War, Drake's
ed., 1829, p. 144.   Morton's Memorial, Davis's ed., pp. 453, 455.

4. Baylies' Hist. Plymouth, pt. 3, 190.   Morton's Memorial, Davis's ed., p.
455.

5. Hubbard's Indian Wars, ed. of 1865, v. 2, p. 37. Morton's Memorial, Davis's
ed., p. 193.   Hutchinson's Hist. Mass., v. 1., ed. of   , p. 307.

the Indians who fled for protection to Rhode Island, were sold for nine years; none were sold for life or sent abroad. The Massachusetts authorities complained that the Rhode Islanders had refused to deliver them up on their demand, that they might "be proceeded against according to the covenant."[1]

Drake's Indian Chronicle consists of reprints of rare tracts and letters written and published during those early times. It is valuable, not so much for its exactness of detail, as for its exposition of the mixture of piety and savageness which actuated the Puritan people; and it gives us some facts additional to those we have.

Captain Mosely took prisoners a father and son. They were examined separately; the father first. They then examined the son, and lied to him by telling that they had shot his father and threatened that they would shoot him if he did not confess; and ended by shooting them both.[2] In another case they led an Indian to the gallows, flung the end of the

1. R. I. Col. Rec., v. 2, p. 240. Knowles's Life of Roger Williams, p. 347. Potter's Early Hist. Narragansett, pp. 94, 219.

2. Drake's Indian Chronicle, ed., 1836, p. 25; ed., 1867, p. 149.

rope over the post and "hoisted him up like a dog three or four times," and finally an Indian stabbed him and sucked his blood.[1]

Eight Indians came to Boston on an embassy with a certificate from Captain Smith.[2]   One of them was taken and hanged, because he had killed some one in the war.[3]

In 1637, the Puritan soldiers meeting with seven Pequods, killed five of them, and took one a prisoner alive, him "the English put to the torture, and set all their heads upon the fort."[4]   The particulars of this torture are not given.   In July, 1676, their Mohegan allies asked the English to give up to them one of the Narragansett captives to be tortured. The English consented.   The remainder of the story is too horrible to be related here, the curious reader is referred to Baylies' History of Plymouth, an excellent authority, pt. 3, p. 136.   The dead body of the squaw Sachem Weetamore being found, her head was cut off and carried to Taunton, where it

1. Drake's Indian Chronicle, ed. 1836, p. 27; ed. 1867, p. 153.
2. Major Richard Smith, well known in Rhode Island history.
3. Drake's Indian Chronicle, ed. 1836, p. 30; ed. 1867, p. 157.
4. Winthrop's History of New England, ed. of 1826, v. 1, p. 223.

was set upon a pole.[1] " We cannot," says Judge
Davis, " peruse without humiliation and disgust the
unfeeling sarcasms with which a reverend cotempo-
rary historian relates this occurrence." [2]

In the Pequod war, the English attacked and set
on fire the Pequod fort, and destroyed about four
hundred Indians, killing some, hewing some to
pieces, etc.   " At this time it was a fearful sight
to see them thus frying in the fire, and the streams
of blood quenching the same.   Horrible was the
stink and scent thereof; but the victory seemed a
sweet sacrifice and they gave the praise thereof to
God, who had wrought so wonderfully for them,
thus to enclose their enemies in their hands." [3]

When the Indians took female prisoners at Lan-
caster, and they suffered no wrong, such treatment
so surprised the Puritan savages that they were
obliged to account for it by a special interposition of
God.[4]   Baylies in his History of Plymouth, says " all
accounts concur in representing the Indians of New

1. Hubbard's Indian Wars, ed. of 1865, v. 1, p. 264.
2. Morton's Memorial, Davis's ed., p. 451.
3. Morton's Memorial, Davis's ed., p. 189.
4. Hubbard's Indian Wars, ed. 1865, v. 2, p. 260.

England to have invariably respected the honor of women." [1] Whatever of a savage character the Indians did, was attributed to "the malicious hatred these infidels have to religion and piety."

In 1646, the Council of the United Colonies, Rhode Island not being one, considering the wilful wrongs and hostile practices of the Indians, and their entertaining and protecting offenders, etc., provided that the magistrates of either of the jurisdictions may send "some convenient strength of English," and seize and bring away any of that plantation of Indians that shall protect," etc., "women and children to be sparingly siezed, unless known to be someway guilty, and because it will be chargeable keeping Indians in prison, and if they escaped, they will be more violent and dangerous," satisfaction is to be again demanded of the Sagamore, and if denied, the magistrates are to "deliver up the Indian siezed to the party or parties endammaged, either to serve or bee shipped out and exchanged for

1. Baylies' History Plymouth, pt. 3, p. 36. Potter's Early History Narragansett, p. 94. Drake's Indian Chronicle, ed. of 1836, p. 81. Hubbard's Indian Wars, p. 117.

Reference might properly have been made in this connection to the treatment of Mary Dyer, who was banished and finally hanged on account of her

neagers as the case will justly beare."[1]   Hazard has modernized the spelling into negroes.

The Commissioners of the United Colonies approved and authorized the employment of mastiff dogs against the Indians.[2]

And read the following : " Whereas Mr. Pincheon was questioned about imprisoning an Indian at Agawam, whipping an Indian and freezing of him, the Court is willing to pass over Mr. *Plums'* failings against an Indian." This is a vote of the General Court at Hartford, in 1637.[3]

When we read of such barbarities as we have recited, and then reflect that these were the Indians who protected our ancestors when they were driven away by the bigoted white savages of our neighboring colony, and when we reflect that these wars and brutalities were brought upon them mainly because of this kind treatment of our forefathers, an old

religious faith, or perhaps, in the estimation of the Massachusetts authorities, the lack of it. The curious scholar is referred to Bishop's New England Judged, for an account of these barbarous acts.

1. Hazard's Historical Collections, vol. 2, page 63. Trumbull's Connecticut Records, 1636–65, p. 531. Blue Laws, Andrus's ed., p. 55.

2. Hazard's Historical Collections, vol. 2.

3. Trumbull's Connecticut Records, 1636–65, p. 13.

fashioned Rhode Islander may be excused for expressing himself in terms of severity.

And yet within a few years we have had a lecture before our Rhode Island Historical Society, ridiculing these our benefactors, and justifying the Puritans. Canonicus is represented as allowing Williams to "instruct his people in Christian decency and behavior, so long as his supply of groceries lasted." And this was received with apparent gratification and a vote of thanks passed by the Society. How long will it be before they join in the annual grand blarney celebration at Plymouth, and sing hosannas to the Puritans, who whipt, scourged and hung our Quaker and Baptist ancestors.

That the Narragansett Indians were not civilized in the Puritan sense is no doubt true. But they were, compared with the other tribes, an agricultural people. And we have the testimony of Roger Williams to their good and peaceable character, (A. D. 1654) : that they were " more friendly in this than our native countrymen. *   * Have they not entered leagues of love and to this day continued peaceable commerce with us? Are not our families

grown up in peace among them?" "The Narragan-
setts as they were the first, so they have been long
confederates with you; they have been true in all
the Pequod wars to you.   *   *   *   The Nar-
ragansetts had never stained "their hands with any
English blood, neither in open hostilities nor secret
murders.   *   * It is true they are barbarians,
but their greatest offences against the English have
been matters of money or petty revenging of themselves on some Indians on extreme provocations, but
God kept them clear of our blood.   *   * Through
all their towns and countries, how frequently do
many and oft times one Englishman travel alone
with safety and loving kindness."[1]

"Commonly they never shut their doors day nor
night, and 'tis rare that any hurt is done."[2]   That
they were corrupted afterwards by their intercourse
with the whites, and that they were made more savage by the treatment they received, is doubtless
true.

Governor Hopkins, in his history of Providence,[3]

1. Potter's Early History of Narragansett, pp. 154, 156 157.
2. Williams's Key to Indian Language, vol. 1, R. I. Hist. Col., p. 50.
3. Massachusetts Historical Collections, second series, vol. 9, p. 202.

speaking of the execution of Miantonomo by the advice of the Puritan clergy, says : " This was the reward he received for assisting them some years before in their war with the Pequods. Surely a Rhode Island man may be permitted to mourn his unhappy fate and drop a tear on the ashes of Miantinomo, who, with his uncle Canonicus, were the best friends and greatest benefactors the colony ever had. They kindly received, fed and protected the first settlers of it, when they were in distress and were strangers and exiles, and all mankind else were their enemies, and by this kindness to them, drew down upon themselves the resentment of the neighboring colonies."

The late Chief Justice Staples, one of the most painstaking and accurate of our antiquarians, who resorted to the records for his facts, and not like some modern lecturers to the imagination for them, says of him : " If he had not protected the first settlers of the State of Rhode Island, probably his liberty would not have been deemed inconsistent with the safety of the United Colonies. * * He was sacrificed because he was more liberal in his views than his Christian neighbors, more benevolent. in his actions, more catholic in his religion. His memory should be embalmed in the grateful recollections of every inhabitant of the State of Rhode Island."[1]

And in another work :

"The descendants of the first settlers of Providence, Rhode Island, and Warwick, should ever remember the obligations that their ancestors were under to Miantonomo. * * * When there was no eye to pity and no power to save in the civilized world, Miantonomo was their friend, their protector, their generous benefactor."[2]

Mr. Savage in his notes to Winthrop,[3] says :

" With profound regret I am compelled to express a suspicion that means of sufficient influence could easily have been found for the security of themselves, the pacifying of Uncas and the preservation of Miantonomo, had he not encouraged the sale of Shaomet and Patuxet to Gorton and his heterodox associates."

1. Gorton's Simplicity's Defence. R. I. Hist. Coll., vol. 2, p. 156.
2. Staples' Annals of Providence, 54.
3. Winthrop's History of New England, ed. of 1853, vol. 2, p. 161.

The names of the Puritan magistrates and clergy who perpetrated these outrages, instead of being damned to everlasting infamy along with the bigots and persecutors of all past ages, are still retained in honor upon the calendar of Massachusetts' saints, and an annual ovation performed in their memory. If the wealthy Quakers and Baptists of the present day had one spark of the spirit of their ancestors, or any regard for their memory, they would place a copy of Coit's Puritanism, Sewel's and Gough's histories of the Quakers, and Benedict's History of the Baptists, in every school and village library throughout the land.

It is common to defend the Puritans by saying that their faults were those of the age in which they lived. If this is a good defence, their defenders should have little to say about Archbishop Laud, or the cruelties of Bloody Queen Mary or any Catholic persecutions.

That the old Puritans (clergy and all) bought and sold slaves may be known to some. But it is not so well known that they were probably the first inventors of a fugitive slave law. In October, 1636,

a treaty was made at Boston, with the great Sachem
Miantonomo. It contained nine articles. But, as
the Indians could not understand them perfectly, a
copy of it was sent to Roger Williams, in Rhode
Island, to interpret it to them. This was probably
a fair specimen of their Indian treaties. It is here
referred to for the fifth article, "to return our fugitive servants." [1] In 1643, Massachusetts, Plymouth
and the two Connecticut colonies made a confederation for mutual defence; in 1672, they renewed it.
One of the articles provided that "if any servant
ran away from his master * * in such case upon
the certificate of one magistrate in the jurisdiction
out of which the said servant fled, or other due
proof, the said servant shall be delivered either to
his master or any other that pursues and brings such
certificate or proof." But this solemn agreement it
seems was hardly needed, for in the letters of a French
Protestant Refugee, written in 1687, it is said : "You
may also own negroes and negresses. There is not
a house in Boston, however small, that has not one
or two," some five or six. "Negroes cost from

---

1. Potter's Early Hist. Narragansett, p. 21.

twenty to forty pistoles.   *   *   There is no danger
that they will leave you, nor hired help likewise,
for the moment one is missing from the town, you
have only to notify the savages, who, provided you
promise them something, and describe the man to
them, he is right soon found." [1]

Selling into slavery was not confined to the Indians or the blacks. In 1659, a son and daughter
of Lawrence Southwick were fined for " siding with
the Quakers, and absenting themselves from the
public ordinances." Not paying their fines the county treasurers were authorized to sell them into Virginia or Bermuda.

That the negroes were generally humanely treated
is very probable, but they had little protection from
the laws. Dr. Belknap [3] in 1795, says " the negro
children were considered incumbrances, and were
given away like puppies," and that the severest and
most effective threat to a negro, was that he should
be sold to the West Indies or Carolina.

1. Winthrop's Hist. New England, ed. of 1826, vol. 1, 199.
2. Sewel's History of the Quakers, vol. 1, p. 278. Hinman's Blue Laws, p. 17.
3. Massachusetts Hist. Coll., 1st series, vol. 4, p. 200.

In the "Body of Liberties" of Massachusetts, A. D. 1641, we find it enacted : "There shall never be any bond slavery, villanage nor captivity among us, unless it be lawful captives taken in just wars and such strangers as willingly sell themselves or are sold unto us ; and these shall have all the liberties and Christian usages which the law of God established in Israel requires." This legal recognitition of slavery is said to be several years earlier than can be found in the laws of Virginia or Maryland.[1] Of the existence of slavery in Rhode Island, I have written in another place.[2] The Rhode Islanders apprenticed or sold some of the Indians for a term of years in the great Indian war of 1675–6. They sold none absolutely. They did in May, 1659, pass a law authorizing the sale of an Indian guilty of grand larceny, but it was only after conviction and it was the guilty person who was to be sold. Even this is not to be justified, but it is not quite as bad as when one Indian committed a theft, to catch and sell another one.[3]

1. Hildreth's History of United States, vol. 1, p. 278.
2. Lecture before the R. I. Hist. Society by the author, February 19, 1851.
3. Rhode Island Colonial Records, vol. 1, p. 412.

In an act of the Massachusetts Legislature passed in May, 1705, entitled "an act for the better preventing of a spurious and mixed issue," etc, it was enacted that if any negro or mulatto struck a person of the English or other Christian nation he should be severely whipped.   To further illustrate the spirit of the people, the two following extracts from private letters are introduced, the first, from Hugh Peters, was written to John Winthrop, from Salem, probably about 1645.   He says :

"Mr. Endecot and my selfe salute you in the Lord Jesus.   Wee have heard of a dividence of women and children in the bay and would be glad of a share, viz. : a young woman or girle and a boy if you thinke good.   I wrote to you for some boyes for Bermudas which I think is considerable."[1]

The second is from Emanuel Downing, son-in-law of Governor Winthrop.   It was written in 1637–8. He says : "A warr with the Narragansett is verie considerable to this plantation, for I doubt whither yt be not synne in vs, hauing power in our hands, to suffer them to maynteyne the worship of the devill,

---

1. Massachusetts Historical Collections, series 4, vol. 6, p. 95.

which their paw wawes often doe; 2lie. If upon a
Just warre the Lord should deliver them into our
hands, we might easily haue men, woemen and children enough to exchange for Moores, which will be
more gayneful pilladge for us than wee conceive, for
I do not see how wee can thrive untill wee gett into
a stock of slaues sufficient to doe all our business
for our children's children will hardly see this great
Continent filled with people, soe that our servants
will still desire freedom to plant for themselves, and
not stay but for verie great wages. And I suppose
you know verie well how we shall maynteyne 20
Moores (negroes) cheaper than one Englishe servant.

"The ships that shall bring Moores may come
home laden with salt which may beare most of the
chardge, if not all of yt. But I marvayle Conecti-
cott should anywayes hasard a warre without your
helps."[1]

We have seen that while the hatred of heresy was
one source of hostility towards Rhode Island, the
passion for land speculation was another. Roger Wil-

---

1. Massachusetts Hist. Coll., series 4, vol. 6, p. 65.

liams[1] says : " You will find the business at bottom to
be * * a depraved appetite after * * great
portions of land in this wilderness. * * * This
is one of the Gods of New England." Deeds of im-
mense tracts were obtained from the Indians by
Massachusetts men on the one hand, and Rhode Island
men on the other.   Sometimes there was a consideration, sometimes none, and how much the Indians
understood of the nature of a deed may easily be
guessed.   For the manner in which treaties were
forced upon them, and how little they understood of
them, repeated illustrations can be seen in the histories of the times.[2]

The Colonial Magistrates sent for the Indian
Sachems at pleasure, made charges against them and
compelled them to sign writings of the effect of which
they knew nothing.   So King Philip was compelled
to sign a writing acknowledging himself a subject of
the English.   When at Boston, in 1671, he was told
that he had done so, he indignantly denied it,[3] and

1. Potter's Early Hist. Narragansett, p. 162.
2. Potter's Early History of Narragansett, pp. 21, 47, 49, 70.
3. Hutchinson, 1, 281.   Baylies' Plymouth, pt. 3, p. 23.

said that it was merely an agreement of friendship and amity.

Baylies, in his History of Plymouth, gives a character of Philip, very different from that generally given by the clerical historians.[1]

The Rev. Samuel Peters has been very much censured for his history of the first colonists of Connecticut. That he exaggerated the faults and foibles of those whom he considered his persecutors, is very probable. He is commonly understood as representing that they met in solemn meeting and voted unanimously—

1st. That the earth is the Lord's and the fullness thereof.

2d. That he has given it to his saints ; and

3d. That we are the saints,

and accordingly they took possession.

This is rather an exaggeration of what Peters does say, but not much.[2]   He says that when the Sachems refused to give the land to them, they voted themselves to be the children of God, and that the wilderness in

1. Baylies' Plymouth, pt. 3, p. 169.
2. Peters' History Connecticut, New Haven, 1829, pp. 46, 66.

the uttermost parts of the earth was given to them. Be this as it may, nothing better represents the ruling spirit of the Puritans in their treatment of the Indians. It represents what was in the minds of all the people. It is true as a myth, in the sense of the myths of ancient history. The same thing is now going on at the West; except that it is not the fashion of the present day to profess any peculiar sanctity. They ask no leave of God or any body else.

Another charge against Peters is, that he represents the first settlers as meeting and voting that they would be governed by the Laws of God, until they had time to make better ones. What he does say (page 54) is that the Colony "adopted the Bible for its code of civil laws, till others should be made more suitable for their circumstances." This was probably founded on some expression in the first Code of Connecticut, where it appears that they provided for being governed by the rule of the Word of God in cases for which they had not provided in their code;[1] or, as Secretary Hinman states it, "for

1. Trumbull's Hist. Connecticut, vol. 1, p. 98.

want of a law in any particular case, shall be judged by the Word of God."[1]

The Rhode Island code of laws of 1647, is a most excellent one. It contains plentiful references to the laws of England,[2] but no reference whatever to the Laws of God. But then its authors were heretics.

The Puritans perhaps were not the first to bribe members of the cabinet and government officers. They were very cautious and perhaps conscientious as to using such a wicked word. But Puritan shrewdness was equal to the occasion. Chalmers openly charges them with attempting to bribe the officers and influential men of the English government.[3] The Massachusetts Council, December 31, 1663, appointed a committee " to *improve* some friend or friends in England,"[4] to obtain information " and *prevent all inconveniences* the best they

1. Hinman's Blue Laws, pp. 130, 150; also Baylies' History Plymouth, pt. 2 p. 74. Laws of Plymouth.

2. Proceedings of First General Assembly of Rhode Island in 1647, ed. of Judge Staples. Providence, 1847.

3. Chalmers' Political Annals, pp. 412, 413, 461; also History of Revolution of Colonies, vol. 1, p. 132.

4. Massachusetts Colonial Records, vol. 4, pt. 2, p. 101.

may." The General Court, May 18, 1664, referring to this, authorized the committee to engage some faithful friends in England, at an expense not exceeding £400. The General Court had before this in 1661, authorized a committee for managing their affairs at London, to *remove all obstacles* or objections that might lie in their way, and their proceedings were to be kept secret unless the General Court should call for them.[1] In 1682,[2] they had authorized the committee managing their English affairs " to *improve* any *meet instrument* for the obtaining" a general pardon and continuance of their charter.

Hereafter Railroad companies will not wickedly attempt to bribe members of Congress, they need only *improve* them.

Their agents in England, either forged or surreptitiously procured before it had passed the proper ordeal, a pretended patent bearing date in 1643,[3] giving to Massachusetts the government of the Narragansett country, including of course the site of our

1. Massachusetts Colonial Records, v. 4, pt. 2, p. 39.
2. Chalmers' Political Annals, p. 461.
3. Miscellaneous State Papers, v. 1. Secretary of State of Massachusetts.

Frenchtown settlement. Of this pretended patent
Roger Williams says :[1] "The Lord High Admiral
President said openly in a full meeting of the Commissioners, that he knew no other charter for these
parts than what Mr. Williams had obtained, for he was
sure that charter which the Massachusetts Englishmen pretended, had never passed the table." For
other reasons and authorities, see Mr. Aspinwall's
pamphlet[2] upon this subject. No one pretends that
the government of Massachusetts would procure or
countenance a forgery. It was a clique of unprinci-
pled land speculators acting under the cloak of their
name and under the garb of piety and hatred of
heresy. And this was the sort of people who caused
a very large part of the conflicts and civil disturb-
ances which hindered and delayed the peaceable settlement of Narragansett, and of which Rhode Island
has had most unjustly to bear the blame.

The feeling produced by these arrogant assump-
tions, by these scourgings, banishings, hangings of

1. Letter to Mason. Potter's Early History Narragansett, pp. 37, 161. See
also the documents in Staples's ed. of Gorton's Simplicity's Defence, p. 205, 195.

2. This exhaustive argument was re-published by Sidney S. Rider, Providence, 1865. A few copies yet remain unsold.

our heretical ancestors has not yet entirely disappeared among the older portion of our country people. And it ought not to, so long as the authors of these barbarities are defended and canonized as they are. I have in my youth seen elderly people who could not speak of the "Massachusetts Presbyterians," as they called them, without a gritting of teeth.

We have had a few among our people who have taken some pains to justify the memory of our ancestors. The late Hon. Henry Bull of Newport, was one of the first, and latterly, Benedict in his History of the Baptists, the late Judge Staples, Governor Arnold in his History of Rhode Island, Zachariah Allen, Esq., and Professor Diman, have done good service in bringing to light the truth on these subjects.

The conduct of the Puritans and the savage character of their treatment of the Indians, will by many be justified on the theory that they could not be dealt with in any other manner. Whether this excuse is available for a people pretending to Christianity is doubtful. That after the Great Swamp fight both parties acted like savages, is undeniable. The Indians had been nearly destroyed in the fight, their huts with their women and children, and their stores of provisions burnt up, and the survivors driven out in the cold of mid-winter to freeze and starve.

On the part of the whites the fury extended even to the women. The women of Marblehead, coming out of church, fell on two Eastern Indians who had been brought in as captives and "very barbarously" murdered them.[1] And very lately a monument has been erected (as the newspapers say) to a woman who tomahawked and scalped ten sleeping Indians and then escaped. The wars with the Eastern Indians were going on at the time of Philip's war.

It is becoming the fashion to erect monuments to the dead Indians, now that they are out of the way and can give us no trouble. Matthew xxiii., 30; Luke ix., 59 : 60.

1. This occurred in 1677. See Hutchinson's Massachusetts Bay, vol. 1, p. 307.

GENEALOGICAL NOTES.

WHEN, many years ago, the writer was collecting materials for the " Early History of Narragansett" published in 1835, it was with the utmost difficulty that the materials could be obtained for the few pages of family history contained in that work. Few families had preserved any family records, and few seemed to care about them. And most of the information in that work was obtained from the records with a good deal of labor. From one person, the late Thomas B. Hazard, of Peace Dale, who died A. D. 1845, at the of age 90, he obtained a great deal of traditional information about Mr. Hazard's own, and other families, which in every instance he found to be confirmed by the records, when searched.

Since then the feeling has changed; every family has some one engaged in hunting up its history, and the passion has been carried to a ridiculous extreme. Those who get up the present fashionable genealogies begin away back in English history with an account of all the princes, lords and knights who have borne the name or any name similar to it.   We expect, of course, to find the descendants of some of these nobles coming over about 1620, and settling in this country.   But here comes a sudden break; and the family history begins again generally somewhat in this style: The first of the name we find in this country was ———. A few years ago some one published a genealogical table of one of our old families, and represented his ancestor as owning almost the whole country.   Such things as these may flatter vanity, but they subject the writers, justly, and sometimes a whole family unjustly to censure.

Savage, in his Genealogical Dictionary, volume 4, page 144, well says: " Much benefit to thousands of enquirers on our side of the ocean may be derived from the wise use of a few words in the note of Mr. Hunter, on pages 6 and 7 of ' The Founders of New Plymouth,' edition 1854: ' Mere possession of a surname which coincides with that of an English family,

is no proof of connection with that family.   Claims
of alliance founded on this basis are not the legiti-
mate offspring of laborious genealogical enquiry, but
of self love and the desire to found a reputation for
ancestorial honor, where no such honor is really due.'
Well is the topic explained in further remarks,
founded on experience of more than one gross case
of indecent pretension."

It was formerly very common for sea captains and
travellers to go to the Herald's office, in London, and
procure copies of coats of arms of some one of their
name.   These were brought home and sometimes
framed and conspicuously displayed, and may hereafter perhaps be used as evidence of connection with
the English family.   They are of course worth but
little.

There are but two families in this part of the country, who, to the knowlege of the writer, can trace
their families into Europe for many generations before the emigration.   The family of Dr. John Clarke,
the colonial agent, can, upon undoubted evidence,
go back several generations in England.   Its repre-
sentatives are still numerous in South Kingstown

and Westerly; and the Bernons were of an ancient
and honorable family in Rochelle, in France.

One great difficulty in tracing by our records, arises
from having sometimes many of the same Christian
name living at the same time. In the Reynolds,
Gardner, Hazard and Babcock families, this is
especially the case. In such cases the tracing of the
title to some tract of land, may aid materially. A
very complete genealogy of the Brenton family can
be made from the Land Records of South Kingstown.

Another difficulty arises from the various removals
of families from one town to another. In this respect the Quaker Records afford great aid as to the
members of that society. The general course of
emigration was through Massachusetts to Portsmouth
and Newport, and from thence across to the west
side of the Bay. The Misquamicott settlement
originated in Newport. The settlers had to pass a
wilderness, and the name they gave it, Westerly, is
significant of the state of the country at the time.

After the close of our Revolutionary war, and in
fact ever since, there has been a very large emigration from the Narragansett country to the Western

States. The greatest number of the early emigrants went to Vermont, to the borders of Hoosic River in New York, to the Genesee country, in which name was then included all the country around the small lakes in western New York, to Wyoming and Wilkesbarre, and the borders of the Susquehannah River, and to Marietta in Ohio. And from thence their descendants have become scattered all over the Western States. There was also quite a large settlement of French from Rhode Island near Chatham Four Corners and Hudson, in New York.

THE MAWNEY FAMILY.

———◆———

LE MOINE. The christian name of the first Le
Moine is not given on the plat, but by the tradition
in the family, it was Moses. The French settlers,
according to the family tradition, settled around a
spring on the present Mawney farm, and planted an
orchard there, always since known as the French
orchard, and, within the remembrance of the writer,
there were trees there supposed to be remains of the
original orchard. When the settlement was broken
up, the Mawneys must have remained there; as the
name of Peter Money is on the oldest plat of East
Greenwich known to be in existence, and attached to
the tract of land which has been in the family ever
since. The name seems to have been first changed
to Money, and later to Mawney. The same tradition
preserves the names of two children of Moses:

First, Peter; and second, Mary, who married an Appleby, of New York.

Col. Peter Mawney lived the greater part of his life in East Greenwich, but removed to Providence before his death, and his will is recorded there. He died in Providence, September 9, 1754, aged 65, and is buried, with other relatives, in the old North Burial Ground. This would make his birth about 1689.

He was twice married, first to Mary Tillinghast, who died February 24, 1726-7, in the 34th year of her age, and is buried in the Tillinghast burial ground, next north of the Mawney farm; second, to Mercy, daughter of Pardon Tillinghast, who survived him, and died in 1761, the widow of James Brown, and is buried in the North Burial Ground.

The children of Col. Peter Mawney were:

1. Elizabeth, born November 22, 1714, wife of Joseph Olney.

2. Mercy, married Thomas Fry, Jr., December 23, 1742. In Col. Mawney's will he mentions his granddaughter, Mercy Fry.

3. Lydia, married Dr. Ephraim Bowen, June 10, 1746. See Bowen, post.

4. Mary, married James Angell, October 5, 1752, grandmother of the late Prof. William G. Goddard.[1]

5. John, born August 11, 1718; died June 13, 1754. See below.

6. Pardon, born October 5, 1753; went to sea and never heard from.

7. Sarah, married Joseph Whipple. Their son Samuel was father of the late Hon. John Whipple, Brown University, 1802, and their son George was grandfather of Joseph W. Congdon, attorney at law at East Greenwich.

8. Amey, married Dr. Samuel Carrew, April 22, 1760; died 1762, age 26; buried in North Burial Ground.

John Mawney, son of Col. Peter, died before his father, and his will is recorded in Providence. He married, October 29, 1745, Amey, daughter of Robert Gibbs, who is described on his tombstone in the North Burial Ground, as descended from the family of Sir Henry Gibbs, of Dorsetshire, England.

1. Updike's Narragansett Church, p. 155.

Amey, wife of Robert Gibbs, was daughther of Col. Joseph Whipple, and widow of —— Crawford. The children of John and Amey Mawney were :

1. Pardon, born at Providence, December 27, 1748 ; died on the homestead, in East Greenwich, given him by his grandfather's will, August 6, 1831. He married Experience, daughter of Caleb Gardner, of South Kingstown. See below.

2. Dr. John Mawney, a physician, sometime sheriff of Providence county, and was in the expedition that burnt the Gaspee. He died in Cranston, in March 1830, in his 80th year, and was buried in the North Burial Ground. He married, first, Nancy Wilson ; second, Elizabeth Clarke. Children :

a. John, married Ruth, daughter of John Gladding, and left one child, Elizabeth, who . married William A. Cole, and now resides in Shakopee, Minnesota.

b. Mary, daughter of John and Elizabeth, married Henry Valentine, A. D. 1807. Their children were, first, Maria A. ; second, Edward H. ; third, John M. ; fourth, Elizabeth ; fifth, Horatio ; sixth, Harriet A. ; seventh, Alfred A., now in New York city. Mrs. Mary Valentine died in Brooklyn, N. Y., 1864. Henry Valentine died in 1847.

c. Susan, born January 5, 1788; married Benjamin P. Ware, 1812. He died in 1816. She died October, 1869. Of the children, Albert P. Ware, born August 3, 1813, is now living in Andover, Massachusetts, and Charles M. Ware, born August 23, 1815, is living at Norwich, Connecticut.

3. Hannah, daughter of John Mawney, married Stephen Harris, January 23, 1775. She died at the age of 34, leaving one son, Stephen, father of the late Almoran Harris.

4. Mary died December 25, 1757, aged eleven years.

5. Nancy died, aged seventeen years.

Pardon, before referred to, died at East Greenwich, August 6, 1831. His wife, Experience, was born November 1, 1751; married June, 1772. She died November 28, 1815. Their children were:

1. Peter Lemoine, born April 16, 1773; died in Moreau, Saratoga county, New York, January 30, 1868. Children: First, John G., died at Tyrone, Steuben county, 1837; second, Pardon, deceased;

third, Horatio, (Geneva, N. Y.) ; fourth, Isabella Ann ; fifth, Sarah ; sixth, Peter, deceased. John G. left children : First, Dr. John G., Mazomanie, Dane county, Wisconsin; second, Caleb; third, William W., Dundee, Yates county, N. Y. ; fourth, Zeruah ; fifth, Mary ; sixth, Sarah ; seventh, Robert.

2. John G., born October 1, 1774, was for many years clerk of one of the courts of Kent county. He died December 28, 1846. Children: First, Mary ; second, William ; third, Tabitha ; fourth, Benjamin ; fifth, Robert G. ; sixth, Julia, married Ebenezer Hopkins ; seventh, John G. ; eighth, Harriet, married Oliver A. Weeks, died October, 1875.

3. One unnamed.

4 and 5. Amey and Nancy, born March 23, 1777. Nancy died 1787. Amey married first, Capt. William E. Tillinghast, of Providence. He died 1817. Second, Elisha Atkins, of Providence, and afterwards of Newport. B. U. 1816. No children. She died October 3, 1864.

6. Mary, born April 24, 1779 ; married, July 9, 1810, Elisha R. Potter, of South Kingstown, member of Congress, 1796–1797 and 1809–1815. She

died July 26, 1835. He died September 26, 1835. Children: First, Elisha R., H. C. 1830; second, Thomas; third, Dr. Thomas M., B. U. 1834, U. S. Navy; fourth, William Henry, B. U. 1836, attorney at law; fifth, James B. Mason, B. U. 1839; sixth, Mary Elizabeth.

7. Moses, born November 4, 1780; married Elizabeth Arnold, November 1816; died August 1, 1821. Children: First, Robert G.; second, Hannah, married Joseph R. Arnold; third, Elizabeth Ann.

8. Hannah, born April 13, 1782; married first, Nicholas Tillinghast. One son, Edward N., born September 11, 1805. Married, second, Jeffrey Davis, December, 1824. She died Sept. 20, 1860.

9. Elizabeth Cranston, born July 7, 1784; married October 19, 1806, Jeffrey Davis, of North Kingstown. She died July, 1814. Children: First, Abby, married Thomas B. Wilbor, of Coventry; second, George Albert; third, William Dean, who married Mary E. Congdon.

10. Nicholas G., born March 18, 1786; died August 27, 1874, on the homestead; unmarried; will recorded at East Greenwich.

11. Robert Gibbs, born 1788; went to sea in 1811 and never heard from.

12. Caleb, born 1789; died 1790.

13. Tabitha, born 1791; died 1808.

14. Samuel Ayrault, born May 8, 1792; married, in 1816, Phebe Nichols; died January 8, 1866. Children: First, Elizabeth, married Edward Wheeler, Auburn, New York; second, Maria, married Maynard Chappell, Henrietta, New York; third, Isabella Ann, married James G. Maynard, Providence, Bureau county, Illinois.

15. Isabella A., born November 30, 1797; married Peter G. Taylor, June 27, 1822; he died at Brooklyn, New York, December 20, 1871; she died July 29, 1873. Children: First, Pardon L., born 1824, died November, 1860, at Brooklyn, New York; second, Isabella Ann, born 1826, married, 1848, George W. Frost, of New Market, New Hampshire; third, Amey Elizabeth, born 1831, married Walter J. Gilbert.

The account of the French settlers here given, the locality of the settlement and the name of the first emigrant of the Mawney family, together with the early history of the family, were taken down by an uncle of the writer from the lips of Pardon Mawney a few years before the death of the latter, in 1831; and when it is considered that Pardon Mawney was born in 1748, and was soon old enough to have conversed with some of the emigrants themselves, and with their families, the tradition becomes more than ordinarily reliable.   Pardon Mawney's grandfather, who died after the birth of Pardon, must have been born in 1689, about the time of the settlement. And until within comparatively a few years there has been very little change in the families which have owned the land and lived in the neighborhood.

Pardon Mawney was for many years in his youth in the house of his uncle Gibbs, in Boston, and while there attended school.   It was during his residence there that Gov. Hutchinson's house was sacked by the mob, in August, 1765; and he was present when the furniture was thrown from the windows, and picked up among the rubbish a pack of playing cards representing scenes in the famous Rye House Plot, which are still preserved.

THE BOWEN FAMILY.

Dr. Ephraim Bowen, son of Thomas, died 1812, age 96 years. Married, first, Mary, daughter of Thomas Fenner, February 9, 1737–8. Second, Lydia, daughter of Col. Peter Money, June 10, 1746. Children by first wife:

1. Gov. Jabez, born November 17, 1739; died in 1815; married, December 19, 1762, Sarah, daughter of Obadiah Brown. She died March 17, 1800.

Children: *a*. Obadiah, born 1763; died 1793. *b*. Oliver, born 1767. *c*. Mary, born 1772. *d*. Jabez, born 1774. *e*. Henry, born 1776; died 1777. *f*. Horatio G., born 1779; Librarian of Brown University; died March 23, 1848. *g*. Another, born 1782. *h*. Henry, 2nd, born 1785; for thirty years Secretary of State of Rhode Island.

He married, second, Peddy Leonard, May 21, 1801. '

2. Oliver, born November 17, 1742. His son, Oliver, Jr., was father of Mary Demont Bowen, lately deceased.

Children by second wife:

3. Dr. William, born March 8, 1747, married Susan Corlis, 1769, died 1832, aged 86 years. Children: *a.* Elizabeth, married Thomas Amory, 1799, whose children were: Mary; Harriet, married Robert H. Ives; John; Julia, married Rt. Rev. M. A. D'W. Howe; Louise; Anna; Helen, married William Raymond Lee; Thomas. *b.* Sarah, married William S. Skinner, 1816. *c.* Maria, married Hon. John Whipple, B. U., 1802, whose children were: John; Maria, married Rev. Francis Vinton; Elizabeth, married Prof. William Gammell; Sarah C. married, first, Robert P. Swann, of Virginia; second, William H. Potter; Samuel, died young; Harriet, married William S. Slater; William. *d.* Harriet, married, 1815, Commodore Charles Morris, United States Navy, whose children were: Charles; Harriet, married Rev. Dr. Coolidge; Louise, married William W.

Corcoran, of Washington; Elizabeth, married Dr. John L. Fox; Helen; R. Murray; Dr. William B. ; Maria, married Rev. Mr. Duncan; George; Julia, married Dr. Addison. *e.* Dr. William C. Bowen, born June 2, 1785; died 1815; married Rebecca Olney, 1812; had a son William.

4. Mary, born 1748; unmarried.

5. Sarah, born 1750; married Thomas Lloyd Halsey.

6. Lydia, born 1752; married John Innes Clarke, 1773, of whose daughters, Harriet married, 1811, Dr. Robert Hare, of Philadelphia, and Anna E., married, 1803, Oliver Kane.

7. Col. Ephraim, born 1753; married, first, Sally Angell; was in the Revolutionary army, and one of the captors of the Gaspee. Children: First, William B., born in 1777, died August 26, 1826. Second, Julia, born in 1779; married John D. Martin, 1803. Third, Nathaniel, died young. Fourth, Sally A., died young. Fifth, Elizabeth, born in 1787; married Hon. John H. Clarke, B. U. 1809, afterwards Senator in Congress. Mr. Clarke died in 1872. Their son, Hon. James M. Clarke, B. U. 1838, was

for several years U. S. District Attorney in Rhode Island.

Col. Bowen married, second, Sarah Whipple in 1794. Children: First, Esther; second, George T.; third, Sarah; fourth, Mary.

Col. Bowen died September 2, 1841, at his home at Pawtuxet, in Warwick.

8.   Benjamin, born 1755.

9.   Dr. Pardon, born March 26, 1757; died October, 1826, age 69 years; married Elizabeth Ward, 1780. Had two sons, William, who went South, and Henry, who died young; and three daughters, Esther, married Charles W. Greene, 1806; Frances, who married Charles W. Greene, 1813, and Anna E., who married Franklin Greene, and is still living at East Greenwich.

10.   Benjamin, born 1759; went to New York.

11.   Ann, born 1762; married Edward Mitchell, 1792. Mrs. Mitchell died in Charleston, S. C., in 1855.

12.   Betsey, born 1765; married John Ward, 1792; no children.

13.   Fanny, 1768; married John E. Moore, 1789.

Dr. William Bowen, Dr. Pardon Bowen, and Dr. William C. Bowen, were all of great eminence in their profession. See Thatcher's New England Medical Biography and Dr. Usher Parsons' Sketches of Rhode Island Physicians.

THE AYRAULT FAMILY.

In Mrs. Lee's Huguenots in France and in
America,[1] Dr. Pierre Ayrault is spoken of as
a native of Angers, in France. He will be at
once recognized as the author of the memorial relating to the breaking up of the French settlement.
Like the Mawneys and other families, he remained
and continued on good terms with the neighboring
Rhode Island settlers, thus showing that the disturbance could have grown out of no national antipathy.
He probably soon removed to the neighboring village
of East Greenwich, as more convenient for his pro-
fessional practice. And in 1699[2] we find him joining
with others in the foundation of Trinity Church, in
Newport, where the petitioners are spoken of as
"within this island." This, however, is not conclu-

1. Mrs. Lee's Huguenots, volume 2, page 108.
2. Arnold's History of Rhode Island, vol. 1, p. 559.

sive. In 1704 Madame Knight, in her journeyings south from East Greenwich, on towards New York, speaks of being joined by the French doctor. In 1711-12 we find from the records at East Greenwich, that Daniel Ayrault sold to David Greene his house and nineteen acres of land. This probably was the time of the final removal of the family to Newport.

Peter Ayrault's will, made in 1705, proved June 4, 1711, and recorded in the old parchment book at East Greenwich, mentions his wife Frances, and his son Samuel, mariner now abroad, giving to the latter a legacy, and giving the remainder of his property to his son Daniel, merchant.

Daniel, the only son of Pierre of whom we have any mention, was born about 1676-7 and settled in Newport. In the old parchment book of records at Greenwich, we find that Daniel Ayrault, with a number of others, received letters of denization July 3, in the thirteenth year of William Third, A. D., 1702. He married, May 9, 1703, Mary, daughter of ———— and Judith Robineau, and grand-daughter of Elias and Susanna Neau, of New York. Their marriage contract, dated

April, 1703, is given at length in Mrs. Lee's Huguenots in France and America.[1] Daniel died June 25, 1764, aged 87 years, 9 months and 17 days. She died January 5, 1729, aged 44 years. He married, second, Rebecca, widow of Edward Neargrass, in 1745. The children of Daniel and Mary were:

1. Mary, born at East Greenwich, February 16, 1704; married James Cranston, 1720-1; children, Walter and Mary; married, second, George Goulding, whom she survived, and died in 1764.

2. Pierre, born at East Greenwich, October 4, 1705.

3. Daniel, born at East Greenwich, November 2, 1707; married, first, Susanna, Neargrass, in 1735; second, Rebecca Neargrass, in 1737; third, Hart, daughter of Jahleel and Frances Brenton, in 1745; she died in 1764. He died in 1770. Children: *a.* Stephen. *b.* Daniel, died young. *c.* Mary, died 1792. Children by Hart Brenton: *a.* Peter; *b.* Hart; *c.* Rebecca; *d.* Martha, born in 1759, died same year, and three others who died young. Peter and Hart both died unmarried.

1. Mrs. Lee's Huguenots, volume 2, page 107.

4.   Stephen, born at East Greenwich, December 11, 1709. The births of numbers two, three and four, are on record at East Greenwich.

5.   Anthony, born in 1712; died in 1726.

6.   Elias, born at Newport, February 13, 1713-14; went to sea.

7.   Judith, born at Newport, in 1716; died young.

8.   Frances, born at Newport, September 2, 1718; married Walter Cranston, March 26, 1747. She died February 2, 1798.

9.   Samuel, born in Newport, March 22, 1720; died August 11, 1798, and buried at the Tillinghast burying ground, on the farm north of the Mawney farm, in East Greenwich. He is described on his tombstone as a merchant.

10.   Anthony, died when 4 years old.

11.   Susanna, born June 29, 1723; died May 3, 1809.

12.   Judith, born December 9, 1725; died November 26, 1806; married Joseph Tillinghast.

Children of Stephen, fourth child of Daniel and Mary. His tombstone gives his age 84. The Mer-

cury of April 22, 1794, contains a notice of him.
He married, December 23, 1740, Ann, eldest daughter of Peter Bours. She was born April 2, 1724, and
died December 17, 1754.

Children : *a.* Frances, baptized 1747 ; married,
first, in 1767, Edward, son of Gov. Gideon Wanton ;
second, John Piper. *b.* Ann. *c.* Mary, baptized in
1742 ; married, in 1764, George Scott. Mary had
one daughter, Ann, who married, first, William Robinson ; second, Dr. John P. Mann. She died in 1841.
d. Bathsheba, died young.

The children of Edward Wanton and Frances, his
wife, were :   First, Stephen A. ; second, Sarah ;
third, Frances, married William C. Robinson. Their
children were :   *a.* Edward W., born in 1797,
died in 1818. *b.* Stephen A., born in 1799 ; married Sarah, daughter of Jeremiah N. Potter, 1822 ;
was Grand Master of Masons, and died April 7,
1877 in South Kingstown. No children. *c.* Frances
W., died young. *d.* George C., died in 1820.
e. William C. Robinson, born in 1803 ; married
Abby B., daughter of Josiah C. Shaw. He died in
1871.

Mary, daughter of Daniel, 2nd, died 1792. She married Benjamin Mason, 1754. Children: Benjamin, Daniel, Susan and Mary. Benjamin, last named, married Margaret Champlin. Their son, George Champlin Mason, was father of George C. Mason, Esq., now living in Newport.

In Hinman's Records of Wethersfield, Conn., and also in the New England Genealogical Register, volume xv., are mentioned several of this name. From the similarity of Christian names, they were probably relatives of the Rhode Island family.

THE BERNON FAMILY.

——◆——

The person who, from his standing in his native country and his wealth was probably the most conspicuous among the French settlers in Massachusetts and Rhode Island, was Gabriel Bernon. He was born April 6, 1644, of an ancient family at Rochelle, of which city it is traditionary in one branch of the family here, he was hereditary registrar. In anticipation of the troubles he fled to London.[1] He landed in Boston in 1688. He was one of the principal persons concerned in the French settlement at Oxford, Massachusetts, for which we must refer to the very full account in Massachusetts Historical Collections.[1] Quite full accounts of him and much of his correspondence are published in the work last referred to, and also in Updike's History of the

1. Massachusetts Historical Collections, vol. 22, p. 60.

Narragansett Church, and in Mrs. Lee's Huguenots in France and America.

In the very full genealogy of the Bernon family, published in France, the posterity of Gabriel Bernon are not given. But his correspondence with his brother Samuel; with Benjamin Faneuil, (of Faneuil Hall memory,) who married his sister Marie; and with another brother-in-law, Pierre Sanceau, all of whom are mentioned in the printed genealogy, and which correspondence is now in the possession of his descendants, all prove the connection. The genealogy extends back to 1545. The Faneuils after coming to this country returned and lived in France.

Bernon and Fanueil and Louis Allaire were concerned together in various mercantile operations. He remained in Boston about ten years and removed to Newport about 1697. He was one of the first petitioners for the establishment of an Episcopal church in Newport, September 1699,[1] and from this and other similar movements originated the English society for the propagation of the Gospel in foreign parts in 1702. Bernon's first wife, Esther Le Roy,

1. Arnold's History of R. I., vol. 1, p. 559: vol. 2, pp. 76, 116.

died in Newport, June 14, 1710, aged fifty-six years, and her gravestone is still to be seen there. For a short time after the death of his wife he resided in Providence, and then began to make purchases with a view to trade in Kingstown. In those days the great road for travel from Boston to New York followed the shore, and was sometimes known as the Pequot path. Wickford, or as then sometimes called, Updike's Newtown, and Tower Hill, were two of the principal places of business on it. He purchased of Lodowick Updike a wharf lot at Wickford, built a wharf, a warehouse, and a sloop.[1] While in Kingstown he was active in support of St. Paul's Episcopal church, of which Rev. James McSparran was rector; but about 1719 we find him again settled in Providence, where he remained until his death.

In 1712 he married for his second wife Mary Harris, daughter of Thomas Harris, 2nd, and grand niece of William Harris the companion of Roger Williams.

Of the children of Bernon's first marriage, Jane married, October 11, 1722, Col. William Coddington, of Newport.

1. Updike's History of the Narragansett Church, p. 42.

Esther married, May 30, 1713, Adam Ap Howell, or Powell.[1] Their daughter Elizabeth, born in Newport, April 8, 1714, married Rev. Mr. Seabury, of New London, whose son Samuel by a former marriage was the first English bishop in America.[2] Esther, (daughter of Adam and Esther Powell,) was born in Newport, May, 1718.[3] She married Judge James Helme, of South Kingstown, and died March 22, 1764, in her forty-sixth year. See Helme family, post. Mrs. Esther Powell died a widow, October 20, 1746, aged sixty-nine years, and was buried in the Congregational burying ground at Tower Hill.

Marie, another daughter of Gabriel Bernon, married Gabriel Tourtellot. See Tourtellot family, post.

Sarah, another daughter, married Benjamin Whipple, November 11, 1722.

Mr. Bernon's eldest son Gabriel and four daughters, children by his first wife, all came with him to America. This son died, unmarried, in early man-

1. Trinity Church Records, Newport.
2. Updike's History of the Narragansett Church, pp. 139, 143.
3. Newport Records.

hood by a shipwreck at the mouth of Narragansett
Bay. In his will, dated February 16, 1727-8, proved
in Providence, February 10, 1735-6, and there recorded, he mentions his former wife, Esther, his
children, Mary Tourtellot, Esther Powell, Sarah
Whipple, and Jane Coddington, and four small
children by his present wife, Mary, viz. : Gabriel,
Susanne, Mary, and Eve : also his son-in-law, Benjamin Whipple. Of their latter children, Gabriel
died young.

Susanne, born 1716, married Joseph, son of William Crawford, August 23, 1734.

Mary Bernon, born April 1, 1719 ; died October
1, 1789 ; married Gideon Crawford, son of William
Crawford. He was born January 29, 1709 ; died
1792. Their daughter Sarah was the first wife of
Capt. Zachariah Allen. Eve Bernon died unmarried.

The location of Bernon's dwelling house in Providence is perfectly well known.[1] It was on the lot
of the original "Roger Williams Spring," on the west
side of North Main street, and next north of his
great grandson, Gov. Philip Allen's house.

---

1. Knowles's Life of Roger Williams, p. 431.

Almost directly opposite Bernon's house was the dwelling of Roger Williams, next to which, though at a later day, was King's Church, now St. John's.

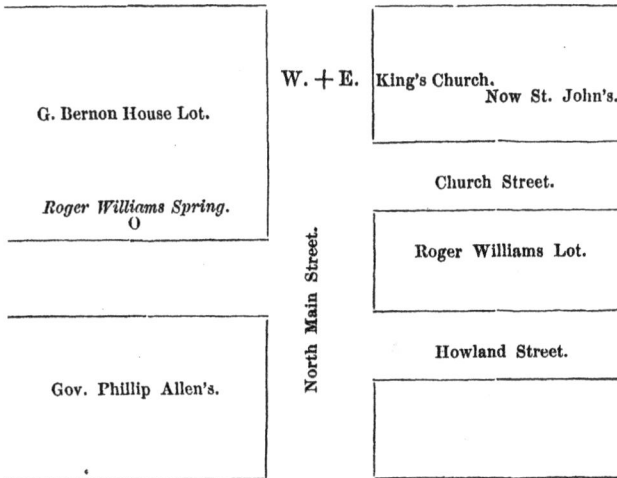

```
┌─────────────────────┐        ┌─────────────────────┐
│                     │ W. + E.│ King's Church.      │
│                     │        │          Now St. John's. │
│ G. Bernon House Lot.│        │                     │
│                     │        └─────────────────────┘
│                     │                  Church Street.
│ Roger Williams Spring.│      ┌─────────────────────┐
│        O            │       │ Roger Williams Lot. │
├─────────────────────┤  North Main Street  │       │
│                     │       └─────────────────────┘
│                     │                  Howland Street.
│                     │       ┌─────────────────────┐
│ Gov. Phillip Allen's.│      │                     │
│                     │       │                     │
└─────────────────────┘       └─────────────────────┘
```

At the age of eighty, Mr. Bernon, embarked for Europe, and while in London, was presented at Court.

He died in Providence, R. I., February 21, 1736, aged 92 years, and was buried beneath St. John's Church, which owed its origin to him,[1] and in which

1. Arnold, vol. 2, p. 75.

a bronze tablet is erected to his memory. An
obituary notice of him was published in Boston.
He was a gentleman by birth and estate, and in
leaving his native land the greater part of his
estate was necessarily left behind him; he was
a courteous, honest, kindly gentleman, behaving
himself as a zealous professor of the Protestant
religion and dying in the faith and hope of a Re-
deemer, and with the inward assurance of salvation;
leaving a good name among all his acquaintances,
and by his upright life giving evidence of the power
of Christianity in sustaining him through his great
sufferings in leaving his country and a great estate
that he might worship God according to his conscience. A great concourse of people attended his
funeral, and listened to an agreeable and eloquent
sermon from Psalm 39 : 4, preached by the Rev. Mr.
Brown.

The family of Bernon is registered in the "Historical and Genealogical Dictionary of the families
of ancient Poitou," and it is stated there that the
name has been known and celebrated since the "ear-
liest ages of the French monarchy."

Numerous articles of value preserved among his descendants, go to show the wealth and social standing of Mr. Bernon.

For some of the numerous descendants of Bernon, see the families of Crawford, Allen, Tourtellot, Helme and Carpenter, post.

As the name of Carré is found in the Bernon genealogy it is very probable that Rev. Ezekiel Carré was a relative of Gabriel Bernon.

THE TOURTELLOT FAMILY.

We find on the Frenchtown plat the name of Abraum Tourtellot. He must, therefore, have been in this country in November, 1686.[1] He was engaged in mercantile pursuits, in partnership with his brother Benjamin, who died on a voyage from London to Boston, September 25, 1687, and Abraum was administrator of his brother's estate, the inventory of which would show a considerable trade. He lived at Roxbury, and by his wife, Mary, had two children, Gabriel, born September 24, 1694, and Esther, born June 12, 1696.

The tradition in the Rhode Island family is that they are descended from Gabriel Tourtellot, who was born at Bordeaux, and who married Marie, daughter of Gabriel Bernon, with whom he came

1. Savage's Genealogical Dictionary, vol. 4, p 315.

over from Rochelle. Bernon's will, dated February 16, 1727-8, proved in Providence, February 10, 1735-6, mentions Mary Tourtellot among his children.

They, Gabriel and Mary, had three children, two sons and a daughter. He lived at Newport, and sailed from there, as master of a vessel, and was with his eldest son, (christian name unknown), lost at sea. The daughter married ——— Harding. Abram, the other son, settled in Gloucester, and was a large land owner there. His mother lived with him in Gloucester and died there. He married Lydia Ballard. Their children were:

First, Mary, born March 20, 1721; married ——— Mitchell. Second and third, Lydia and Esther, twins, born January 24, 1723; Lydia married Thomas Knowlton. Esther married Samuel Dunn. Fourth, Abram, born February 27, 1725; married ——— Harris, and settled in Thomson, Connecticut. Fifth, Jonathan, born September 15, 1728; married ——— Williams, and settled in Scituate, R. I. Sixth, Benjamin, born November 30, 1730; married ——— Ballard, and settled in Vermont. Seventh, Sarah, married John Inman.

Abram, son of Gabriel, married, second, January 29, 1743, Hannah Corps, a widow, whose maiden name was Case. They had five children:

1. Stephen, died young, of small pox.

2. William, married Phebe Whitman, of Providence, and settled in Gloucester. Had eleven children: a. Mary. b. Hannah. c. William, married Lydia Eddy; children: Cyrus, Amasa R., now living, Abradia, John and Lydia. d. Barbary. e. Nancy. f. Sarah. g and h. Hope and Mercy. i. Whitman. j. Amey. k. Abram.

3. Jesse, married ——— Angell; settled in Mendon, Massachusetts; ten children.

4. Daniel, married Urana Keech, and lived and died in Gloucester. By his first wife, he had three children: a. Jesse, who was Judge of the Court of Common Pleas. He married ——— Steere. They had twelve children; among them was my old friend and schoolmate, Jesse S. Tourtellot. b. Jeremiah. c. Dorcas, who married Captain ——— Aborn, of Pawtuxet. Their son Robert lives in New York.

5. Anna, married first, ——— Jones; no children; second, Ebenezer White, who had six chil-

dren : *a.* Nancy. *b.* Esther. *c.* Nabby. *d.* Sally. *e.* Frances and *f.* Mary, who was the second wife of her cousin Jesse, and he was her second husband.

Abram, the son of Gabriel, married for his third wife, ——— Williams. No children.

CRAWFORD AND ALLEN FAMILIES.

—————◆—————

Gideon Crawford emigrated from Lanark in Scotland, and settled in Providence about 1670. He married Freelove, daughter of Arthur Fenner, 1687; he died 1702; his grandson, Joseph, born 1712, married, 1734, Susanne, daughter of Gabriel Bernon. Their children were: First, Sarah; second, Joseph; third, Freelove, married John Jenckes; fourth, Susanne, married Samuel Nightingale; fifth, Mary, married Dr. Amos Throop; sixth, Candace, second wife of Capt. Zachariah Allen; seventh, Esther; eighth, Lydia; ninth, Anne, born in 1759; married Capt. Zachariah Allen, (third wife). She died in 1808. He died in 1801.

The children of Capt. Zachariah Allen and his third wife, were:

1. Zachariah, died young.

2. Lydia, born in 1782, married, in 1804, Sullivan Dorr, of Boston. She died in 1859. He died in 1853.

3. Ann, died unmarried in 1859.

4. Philip, B. U. 1803, married, in 1814, Phebe, daughter of Benjamin Aborn. He was Governor of the State, and Senator in Congress. He died in 1865. Mrs. Allen died in 1864.

5. Candace, died in 1860, unmarried.

6. Zachariah, born September 15, 1795. B. U., 1813. Married, May 1, 1817, Eliza Harriet Arnold, daughter of Welcome Arnold. She died August 30, 1873, aged 76. Mr. Allen received the degree of LL. D. from Brown University in 1851.

7. Crawford, B. U., 1815, married, June 5, 1838, Sarah Senter, daughter of Rev. Nathan B. Crocker, D. D. He died April 22, 1872, aged 74.

HELME AND CARPENTER FAMILIES.

———◆———

Rowse Helme, died 1712; his will is on record in Kingstown; his son, Rowse, married Sarah Niles, and died 1751. His children were: First, James, see post; second, Sands, died 1738; third, Rowse; fourth, Nathaniel; fifth, Benedict; sixth, Simeon; seventh, Benedict; eighth, Silas; ninth, Sarah; tenth, ———; eleventh, Oliver; twelfth, Samuel.

James Helme, born 1710; married Esther Powell, grand-daughter of Gabriel Bernon, in 1738. Mr. Helme was elected Chief Justice of the Supreme Court, in 1767, and was a Judge of that Court for many years, and held other important offices. Their children were: First, Esther, born 1740, married Capt. Francis Carpenter, 1767; their son was Willett Carpenter, lately deceased; second, Powell, died 1780, single; third, Rowse J., who was an attorney at law, an account of him is given in Updike's Memoirs of the Rhode Island Bar; fourth, Sarah; fifth, Elizabeth; sixth, James, see post; seventh, Adam, died unmarried; eighth, Samuel, born 1755, for many years Clerk of the Court in Washington county. His son, Powell, married Elizabeth Kenyon, was for many years clerk of the Supreme Court in Washington county, and Town Clerk of South Kingstown, and died October 20, 1861; ninth, Sarah; tenth, Gabriel, died single; eleventh, Nathaniel.

James Helme, son of Judge James, was born 1749–50, married Sarah Clarke, 1777; he died 1824, in South Kingstown. Their children were: First, James, who had children: *a.* James, now living at Woonsocket, married Elmira Allen, of Franklin, Massachusetts.

b. Sarah, married George Rickard, of Providence. They had seven children, of whom four are now living: 1. Sarah; 2. James H., married Abby S. Weld, of Woonsocket; 3. George Silas, married Penina Jackson, of Woonsocket; 4. Elizabeth Estelle.

c. Mercy P., married James B. Ayres, of Yates county, New York. They had two children: 1. Martha Wanton, married, 1st, Sanford W. Kress, of Yates county; 2nd, Jacob Tremper.

d. Jonathan Perry, married Mary, daughter of William James, of Providence. Had three children, only one now living, Anna P., married Leonard O. Smith, of Franklin, Connecticut, and is now living in Philadelphia.

e. Adam Helme, married Ann Cory, living in South Kingstown. Children: Mary E.; Hittie Ann; Adam Powell.

The other children of James, son of Judge James, were: Second, John, who married Susan, daughter of Elisha R. Gardner, and left two daughters: Mary, who married John Wilbur, of Fall River; Ann, who married Thomas Nason, of Woonsocket. After Mr. Helme's death, his widow married Rev. Israel Washburn, a Methodist clergyman. He died at Middleboro' Massachusetts, in 1864.

Third, Bernon, for many years clerk of the Court of Common Pleas in Providence County, died 1826; married Elizabeth Olney, 1811. Had two children:

James Powell, who died 1825, aged eight years; and Mary, who died single.

Fourth, Nathaniel, B. U. 1819; died, 1822, unmarried. Was an excellent clasical scholar, and for several years Instructor in the classical school at Little Rest, now Kingston.

Willett Carpenter, before named, married Elizabeth, daughter of Joseph Case and sister of the late Dr. Benjamin W. Case, of Newport. He inherited the large estate on Boston Neck, which had belonged to the Willetts and owned it at the time of his death. His children were: Powell H., and Rev. James H. Carpenter, of Wakefield, a clergyman of the Episcopal Church. On the Willett farm was the residence of Theophilus Whale or Whaley, supposed to be one of the regicide judges.[1]

1. For full account of the Willett family see Stiles' History of the Judges; Thomson's History of Long Island, and Updike's History of the Narragansett Church.

THE GANEAUX FAMILY.

———◆———

Francis Ganeaux came from Guernsey and settled at New Rochelle, where he died at the age of 103. The name was soon Englished into Gano. Stephen, son of Francis, had several children, of whom Daniel married Sarah, daughter of Nathaniel Britton, of Staten Island, and removed to Hopewell, New Jersey. Their children were: First, Daniel; second, Jane; third, Stephen, died young; fourth, Susanna; fifth, Rev. John Gano, born at Hopewell, July 22, 1777, ordained in 1754. He lived for some time at Frankfort, Kentucky, and died August 10, 1804. He married Sarah, daughter of John Stiles. Children: *a.* John, died in 1764. *b.* Daniel, born Nov. 11, 1758. *c.* Peggy, born in 1760. *d.* Rev. Stephen, born December 25, 1762; settled over the First Baptist Church, in Providence, in 1792.

e. Sarah, born February 4, 1764. *f.* John S. born in 1766. *g.* Isaac Eaton. *h.* Richard Montgomery. *i.* Susanna. *k.* William.

Sixth, Nathaniel; seventh, David; eighth, Sarah.[1]

Rev. Dr. Stephen Gano was thrice married, first to Cornelia Vavasour, October 25, 1782. Of their children, Cornelia V. married Rev. John Holroyd. Margaret H. married Rev. David Benedict, well known as the author of the History of the Baptists.

Second, married Mary Talmadge, August 4, 1789. Of their children, Sally S. married Rev. Peter Ludlow. Maria T. married Rev. Henry Jackson. Clarissa A. married, first, Newton Robbins, and second, James Ludlow.

Third, married Mary Brown, July 18, 1799. Their only child, Eliza Brown, married Joseph Rogers.

1. Benedict's History of the Baptists, vol. 1, pp. 485, 550, and vol. 2, p. 306. Memoir of Rev. John Gano, New York, 1806.

MARCHANT FAMILY.

———◆———

The tradition of this family, as given me by the late Judge William Marchant, is that three brothers came over from Bayonne, in the time of the persecution, one of whom settled, at Cape Cod, one at Barnstable and one at Martha's Vineyard, from which latter place Capt. Huxford Marchant, a sea captain, removed to Newport. His son, Henry, was educated for the bar and began the practice of the law in Newport, in which he attained great eminence. He was for several years a member of the first Continental Congress, and was one of those who signed the Articles of Confederation when adopted. He was Attorney General of the State. Like many others attached to the new government, he had to leave Newport while it was in the possession of the British. He purchased a farm in South Kingstown and lived there for a time.[1] He received the degree of LL. D. from Yale College in 1792, and died in 1796, at which time he held the office of United States District Judge.

His son, William Marchant, graduated at Yale 1792. He resided for a time in Newport and afterwards in South Kingstown, where he died. He held the offices of Judge of the Supreme Court, the Chief Justice of the Court of Common Pleas, and member of the State Senate. He died January 21, 1857, aged eighty-two years. His son Henry was for a long time a manufacturer in Pawtucket, and died in May 1865. William, son of Judge William, is now living on the homestead farm in South Kingstown.

1. See an account of his life in Updike's Memoirs of the Rhode Island Bar.

TARGÉ FAMILY.

On the plat the name of this family is spelled
Targé. In the old deeds and wills of the family in
North Kingstown it is generally spelled Tourgée.
After the breaking up of the French settlement the
family remained in North Kingstown, but just over
the Greenwich line in the immediate neighborhood
of the proposed settlement. It seems from the plat
that a father and son were among the settlers. The
tradition as preserved in the family, gives the names
of Peter and three sons: Peter, John and Philip.
Professor Tourgée, of the Boston Conservatory of
Music, gives me the following, obtained from the
records at Wickford. Children of Peter: First,
Thomas, born December, 1722; second, Philip,
born October, 1724; third, Elizabeth, born 1728;

fourth, Peter, born February 1733; fifth, John, December, 1735.

John died 1812. His son Jeremiah, born December, 1778 and died 1867. His son, Ebenezer, born in Warwick, 1809, died October, 1878, was father of Professor Eben Tourgée, of Boston.

THE LUCAS FAMILY.

This family was of French descent, and was connected with the Hillhouse and Brenton families, and in Narragansett with Matthew Robinson.[1] Augustus Lucas, the first emigrant, married Marie Lefebvre, daughter of Daniel Lefebvre, of Garhere, January 6, 1696, at St. Malo, in Bretagne. She died February 12, 1698, at Newport. He married, second, at Bristol, Barsheba Elliot, September 21, 1704. Their daughter, Barsheba, was born August 27, 1708, and died, the wife of Matthew Robinson, at Kingston, December 21, 1775.

1. Potter's Early History of Narragansett, p. 296, and Updike's Episcopal Church in Narragansett, pp. 230, 505, 506, and the notices of Matthew Robinson and Augustus Johnson in Updike's Memoirs of Rhode Island Bar.

THE JERAULD FAMILY.

In 1742 Dr. Dutee Jerauld, then about thirty years old came from Medfield, Massachusetts, and settled in East Greenwich, and died in July, 1813, aged 91. His parents were Huguenot refugees. His father was a physician. One of his daughters married Samuel Pearce. Their son, Hon. Dutee J. Pearce, resided in Newport, and was a very able lawyer, Attorney General of the State, member of Congress for twelve years, and acquired considerable influence there. See Dr. Greene's History of East Greenwich, and Dr. Parsons' Sketches of Rhode Island Physicians.

THE GINNADO FAMILY.

———◆———

Lewis Ginnado emigrated from France and married in Newport. He died in Exeter, Rhode Island, near Chapman's Mills, May 23, 1795, aged 79. His wife, Sarah, died in 1801. His daughter, Esther, married Gideon Freeborn. Daniel, his son, lived and died near Mumford's Mills. A lot of land there is still known by his name.

Daniel Ginnado's will was proved in South Kingstown, in February 1816. In it he mentions his children, Samuel H., Lewis, Daniel, Joseph D., Susanna Sherman, Dorcas H. and Peggy.

The will of Daniel Ginnado, 2nd, was dated December 1817, and proved in South Kingstown, January 1818. He mentions his wife, Sally G. Ginnado, son, Samuel Slocum Ginnado, and nephews, Daniel and Alfred.

CLOSING NOTE.

Besides the families of whom we have given some account above, there are other families of French descent: The Levalleys, in Warwick; Jacques, Jaquais, Jacowaise; Le Baron; Geoffroy; Tarbox; Bardine, sometimes Englished from Bourdillé.[1] Andrew Nichols emigrated from Ireland, and married a French wife of the name of Petel, and the late John T. Nichols, Sr., of Kingston, was their grandson. Louis Alaire, whose name is on the Frenchtown plat, was probably a relative of Bernon's.[2]

Of the Frenchtown settlers, the following, probably, went South: Collin, Jouet, Moize Lebrun, Legendre, St. Julien, and Legaré.[3]

For the documents from the British State Paper

1. Massachusetts Historical Collections, volume 22, page 81.
2. Bernon Family, and also Savage's Genealogical Dictionary.
3. Mrs. Lee's Huguenots in France and America, volume 2.

Office, including the map, we were indebted to the courtesy of Gen. Schenck, while minister at the Court of St. James. A reduced copy of this is prefixed. The other plat is reduced from the old plat of East Greenwich, and gives the lots as they were held by the settlers under the Rhode Island title.

We are indebted to several ladies and gentlemen for assistance and contributions; and more especially to Mr. Sidney S. Rider, for the great pains he has taken in contributing information and in making the statements, dates, etc., exact. Still, no doubt, errors will be found, as for instance, on page 89 it is related that a company of French settled at Chatham Four Corners, in New York: the word French is an error for Friends, and was not discovered in time to be corrected; and again on page 26, the name Legree should have been Legaré.